finding
FORGIVENESS

finding FORGIVENESS

Discovering the Healing Power of the Gospel

STANLEY D. GALE

Reformation Heritage Books
Grand Rapids, Michigan

Finding Forgiveness
© 2016 by Stanley D. Gale

Reformation Heritage Books
2965 Leonard St. NE
Grand Rapids, MI 49525
616–977–0889 / Fax 616–285–3246
orders@heritagebooks.org
www.heritagebooks.org

Printed in the United States of America
16 17 18 19 20 21/10 9 8 7 6 5 4 3 2 1

Library of Congress Cataloging-in-Publication Data

Names: Gale, Stanley D., 1953- author.
Title: Finding forgiveness : discovering the healing power of the gospel / Stanley D. Gale.
Other titles: Why must we forgive?
Description: Grand Rapids, Michigan : Reformation Heritage Books, 2016. | Expanded edition of author's Why must we forgive? c2015. | Description based on print version record and CIP data provided by publisher; resource not viewed.
Identifiers: LCCN 2016042358 (print) | LCCN 2016041433 (ebook) | ISBN 9781601785039 (epub) | ISBN 9781601785022 (pbk. : alk. paper)
Subjects: LCSH: Forgivenes—Religious aspects—Christianity. | Forgiveness of sin.
Classification: LCC BV4647.F55 (print) | LCC BV4647.F55 G25 2016 (ebook) | DDC 241/.4—dc23
LC record available at https://lccn.loc.gov/2016042358

For additional Reformed literature, request a free book list from Reformation Heritage Books at the above regular or e-mail address.

To my church family for over twenty-eight years,

The Reformed Presbyterian Church
of West Chester, Pennsylvania

CONTENTS

INTRODUCTION

It was the blank pages that did it. That was the impetus for the book you hold in your hand. In 2015 Reformation Heritage Books published a booklet I wrote on the topic of forgiveness as part of their Cultivating Biblical Godliness series. It was titled *Why Must We Forgive?* and briefly dealt with some of the fundamentals of forgiveness, that most basic of Christian graces.

The gospel is conspicuous in power and glory through the practice of forgiveness. Relationships are healed and community strengthened. The grace of forgiveness bears witness to the gospel, and the hope for a better world shines forth. Forgiveness displays the glory of a reconciling God and gives teeth to the angelic announcement: "Glory to God in the highest, and on earth peace, goodwill toward men!" (Luke 2:14).

This is the picture I painted in *Why Must We Forgive?* The booklet covered a good deal of ground, albeit in generally broad strokes because of the brevity of the treatment. I remember first holding the bound, finished product in my hand, always a point of satisfaction for an author. I paged through it, reflecting on all the work that goes into the writing process and editorial gestation of a book, pleased to be able to make a small contribution to the literature on the subject, and praying for its usefulness to Christ's church.

Then I got to the end of what I had written, and there were those blank pages—five of them, a bit glaring for such a small book. It was like they were taunting me, suggesting that I had not adequately addressed the subject, that there was more to be said and I had been remiss by pulling up short of the goal. But that's the way it was—time to move on to the next project. But the first project would not give up so easily.

I am part of a writers' group. Five of us meet monthly to review one another's work and share helpful comments about content, flow, and grammar and generally encourage one another in the writing process. I am the lone religious nonfiction writer. As always, the group was helpful in their writing expertise but also in the questions they raised about forgiveness.

One group member posed a question: What about forgiving ourselves? Evidently, that struck a chord, because the others started to chime in, saying that forgiving ourselves was essential to a proper treatment of the subject. One even went as far as to suggest that self-forgiveness was foundational, something we must come to grips with before we can move on to forgiving others.

There it was, the material for the five blank pages. The problem was that the booklet had already been published.

I contacted Reformation Heritage Books with the idea of a second edition. That conversation generated other dimensions relating to forgiveness that would be helpful to a more thorough study of the subject, moving it from booklet to book format. So my first acknowledgment is to Joel Beeke, editorial director, and to the editorial staff at RHB for their encouragement in the project. A special mention goes to Jay Collier, director of publishing, for his early involvement in bringing the book to life. In addition, Dr. Beeke and Dr. Ryan McGraw, coeditors of the Cultivating Biblical Godliness series, were invaluable in stimulating me to take up certain considerations in dealing with the subject of forgiveness. Annette Gysen, senior manuscript editor for RHB and project editor for my books, helped me to flesh out the practice of forgiveness in addressing specific relationship challenges. Annette is a joy to work with in that she is more than a stylistic taskmaster; she is also an invested reader who interacts with the material to make it richer.

Those of you who have read *Why Must We Forgive?* will experience a sense of déjà vu in that what you read within will sound familiar. I have taken the approach of dividing the content of that booklet and augmenting and illustrating it in greater detail. Sections of that booklet have grown into chapters for this book. Practical matters dealing with the nuts and bolts of forgiving are spread across two chapters, fleshing out various considerations. A full chapter is devoted to the question of the biblical propriety of forgiving ourselves, and why that topic resonates with so many. In that light, I would like to thank those members of my writers' group who inspired discussion on the subject as well as for their help in the art and science of writing and for helping me to keep it real: Audra Supplee, Alexandra Coulter, and Gretchen Lockwood. While another member, Stephen

Thompson, was not part of the conversation about forgiving ourselves, he did contribute to the print worthiness of both the booklet and the book.

My gratitude reaches to new heights in recognizing my wife, Linda, for her contribution to this book, because she has illustrated a forgiving spirit for the forty-plus years of our marriage. She has also served up a ready reminder for me to put into practice the gospel principles I believe and teach, helping me keep the log out of my own eye.

The topic of forgiveness raises many questions, which we address to some degree in the following pages:

1. Is it biblical to "forgive and forget"?

2. Why do we need to confess our sins if they are already forgiven?

3. Does Jesus's parable of the unforgiving servant teach that God's forgiveness can be rescinded?

4. Is it hypocritical to forgive if we don't feel like it, especially when Jesus says we are to forgive from the heart?

5. Why does John say that God is "faithful and just" to forgive us when we confess rather than "faithful and merciful"?

6. Does God forgive sins simply because a person confesses them?

7. When Jesus says, "If your brother repents, forgive him," is He making repentance a pre-requisite for granting forgiveness?

8. How do we actually go about forgiving someone?

9. How is asking for forgiveness different from apologizing?

10. How does forgiveness relate to reconciliation?

11. What does God's forgiveness of us teach us about our forgiveness of others?

12. What does the biblical terminology of forgiveness convey about its tone?

13. Does the Bible give a place to forgiving ourselves?

14. What does life look like after forgiveness?

15. How does forgiveness lead us to the battlefield of spiritual warfare that is constituent to the life of the Christian in a fallen world?

Even though this book addresses those nagging blank pages of the booklet, it will not and cannot be exhaustive. There is always more that could be said, new insight gleaned from the study of God's Word, and fresh apprehension of the glorious gospel of grace. With the application of forgiveness in the healing of a burdened spirit or a broken relationship, the awe of the gospel dawns anew and presents a spectacle of beauty and certain hope of a better life to come for those who know and love Jesus Christ.

I would delight in hearing how the Lord used this book in your life and what questions or topics you might have that carry a discussion of forgiveness further.

—Stan Gale
sdgale@CHOPministry.net

Chapter 1
FORGIVENESS AND THE GOSPEL

I believe…in the forgiveness of sins.
—THE APOSTLES' CREED

Isaiah thought he was going to die. In his vision he found himself in the throne room of the living God. Around the temple sanctum flew angelic beings, seraphim by name. They cried out to one another in chorus, "Holy, holy, holy is the LORD of hosts; the whole earth is full of His glory" (Isa. 6:3). Such was the seismic scene of God's majesty and holiness that the temple was shaken to its foundations. The room filled with smoke, a theophany indicative of the very presence of God.

At this awe-full sight, Isaiah realized that he stood face-to-face before this holy God. It was then that he uttered these words:

Woe is me, for I am undone!
Because I am a man of unclean lips,
And I dwell in the midst of a people of unclean lips;
For my eyes have seen the King,
The LORD of hosts. (Isa. 6:5)

Never had the prophet been more aware of his sin than at that moment, in the presence of pure and majestic holiness. No sinner could stand before God and live. Isaiah was going to die, consumed by the wrath of God.

Not only was Isaiah plunged into an acute awareness of the pollution of his sin and profound dread of judgment for it, he also became painfully aware of his utter hopelessness. There was nowhere to run, nowhere to hide. There was nothing he could do to save himself. Then something remarkable happened, something totally unexpected and wholly undeserved and completely out of Isaiah's control: "One of the seraphim flew to me, having in his hand a live coal which he had taken with the tongs from the altar. And he touched my mouth with it, and said:

> 'Behold, this has touched your lips;
> Your iniquity is taken away,
> And your sin purged.'" (Isa. 6:6–7)

While Isaiah could do nothing to save himself from the just wrath of a holy God, God acted on his behalf. He sent one of the seraphs to the altar. From that place of sacrifice the angel took a burning coal and with it touched Isaiah's lips. In so doing, the angel issued this declaration: "Behold, this has touched your lips; your guilt is taken away, and your sin atoned for." God had dealt with the sin Isaiah could not. God had enabled Isaiah, a sinful man, to stand in the presence of His holiness, without fear. Isaiah's sin and guilt were not ignored; they were resolved.

This scene with Isaiah is one of the many poignant previews of the gospel found throughout the Old Testament, anticipating the reality to come. After the coming of Jesus, Paul presents a similar scenario in laying out the gospel to the church at Rome. The apostle sets the stage by making it clear that every human being, Jew and Gentile, is a sinner unfit to dwell before a holy God and unable to save himself. Not only is no one inclined to seek God, but also there is no avenue by which to merit salvation and escape the wrath of God. Paul says as much: "Now we know that whatever the law says, it says to those who are under the law, that every mouth may be stopped, and all the world may become guilty before God. Therefore by the deeds of the law no flesh will be justified in His sight, for by the law is the knowledge of sin" (Rom. 3:19–20). This condition of every human being is akin to a physician's diagnosis of terminal cancer, spread throughout the body, infecting every major organ. Death reigns. The inevitable awaits. Paul expresses what Isaiah experienced—a terminal condition, a helplessness, and a hopelessness.

At this bleak juncture the apostle issues the glorious and gracious good news of the gospel:

> But now the righteousness of God apart from the law is revealed, being witnessed by the Law and the Prophets, even the righteousness of God, through faith in Jesus Christ, to all and on all who believe. For there is no difference; for all have sinned and fall short of the glory of God, being justified freely by His grace through the redemption that is in Christ Jesus, whom God set forth as a propitiation by His blood, through faith, to demonstrate His righteousness, because in His forbearance God had

passed over the sins that were previously committed. (Rom. 3:21–25)

The holy drama of Isaiah's encounter with God is played out centuries later on the stage of human history. What none could do in their sinfulness, God undertook to do. The means of sin's removal in Isaiah's vision was a burning coal taken from the altar (Isa. 6:7), which anticipates God's remedy for sin described later in Isaiah's prophecy,[1] the One who would be God's answer to how a holy God can be just and the justifier of the ungodly (Isa. 1:18; Rom. 3:26).

In the clarity of prophetic fulfillment, we see that provision for the atonement of sin is Jesus Christ, burning with God's wrath from the altar of the cross, brought to a helpless sinner for propitiation. It is in Christ and Christ alone that it can be said, "Your iniquity is taken away, and your sin purged" (Isa. 6:7).

God saves sinners by dealing with their sin. Paul identifies God's means for sinners to be reconciled to Himself, and the sole reason for it:

But God demonstrates His own love toward us, in that while we were still sinners, Christ died for us. Much more then, having now been justified by His blood, we shall be saved from wrath through Him. For if when we were enemies we were reconciled to God through the death of His Son, much more,

my sin now resolved thank you JESUS

---

1. The eternal Son of God incarnate of a virgin (Isa. 7:14), born to be messianic King (Isa. 9:6–7), who would be given rule and authority through His work as Suffering Servant (Isaiah 42, 49, 53).

having been reconciled, we shall be saved by His life. And not only that, but we also rejoice in God through our Lord Jesus Christ, through whom we have now received the reconciliation. (Rom. 5:8–11)

What Isaiah knew in shadow, we on this side of the cross know plainly and in substance. Every sinner saved by grace who echoes the woeful despair of Isaiah will exclaim the wonder of such a great salvation:

> Guilty, vile and helpless, we;
> Spotless Lamb of God was He;
> Full atonement! Can it be?
> Hallelujah, what a Savior![2]

Good News of Great Joy

Being the bearer of good news is always exciting. My wife, three children, and I were sitting around a table at Burger King. My kids were ages 15, 13, and 11. Going out anywhere to eat was a special treat for us in those days, even to a fast-food restaurant. As we enjoyed our food, my wife, Linda, cryptically said, "I had my doctor's appointment today, and we're both fine." Blank faces. Trying to make sense of her mom's statement, my daughter Samantha asked, "Dad went too?"

Linda: "No, just me."

After several heavy moments of silence, my son Luke blurted out, "You mean you're pregnant?" That's how we

---

2. Philip P. Bliss, "Man of Sorrows! What a Name," public domain.

broke the news that their forty-two-year-old mother was
going to have a baby.

That was exciting news and fun to share, especially to
see the dawning of realization on our kids' faces. How much
more exciting would it be to tell a person whose body is
wracked with cancer and without remedy that a total cure
had been developed and was available? Dire straits would be
swept away by the hope of healing and the promise of restoration to a normal life.

That is why the gospel is both "good" and "news." The
angels in the heavenly throne room of Isaiah's vision were
actors in a redemptive drama that communicated to the
prophet, and to all who would read the account for generations, that forgiveness of sin is provided by the One sinned
against. Eight hundred years later an angel would be dis-
patched from God to shepherds tending their sheep at night
in the Judean countryside outside the town of Bethlehem.
That celestial being had news to bring:

> And behold, an angel of the Lord stood before them,
> and the glory of the Lord shone around them, and
> they were greatly afraid. Then the angel said to them,
> "Do not be afraid, for behold, I bring you good tid-
> ings of great joy which will be to all people. For there
> is born to you this day in the city of David a Savior,
> who is Christ the Lord." (Luke 2:9–11)

Other angels would join this angel in heavenly chorus, prais-
ing God and saying, "Glory to God in the highest, and on
earth peace, goodwill toward men!" (Luke 2:14). Just as God
is acknowledged as holy in the superlative for His being in

Isaiah 6, He is afforded glory in the superlative for such a great salvation—glory to God in the highest.

But while angels served as messengers of the good news of God's salvation in the birth of the Messiah, it is those who actually experience the joy of sins forgiven who are appointed ambassadors of it to each generation ahead:[3]

> Now all things are of God, who has reconciled us to Himself through Jesus Christ, and has given us the ministry of reconciliation, that is, that God was in Christ reconciling the world to Himself, not imputing their trespasses to them, and has committed to us the word of reconciliation.
>
> Now then, we are ambassadors for Christ, as though God were pleading through us: we implore you on Christ's behalf, be reconciled to God. For He made Him who knew no sin to be sin for us, that we might become the righteousness of God in Him. (2 Cor. 5:18–21)

We see that pattern in the account of Isaiah after his experience of God's forgiveness. God asks, "Whom shall I send, and who will go for Us?" Without delay Isaiah says, "Here am I! Send me" (Isa. 6:8). We can almost see his arm shoot up while he bounces on the balls of his feet, like a schoolchild who knows the answer to the teacher's question.

The gospel provides the answer. How can sinners be reconciled to a holy God? The answer is Jesus Christ and Him crucified. How can God be just and the justifier of the

---

3. It was not for angels that Christ came to die (see Heb. 2:14–17).

ungodly? The answer is Jesus Christ, who took on Himself the sin of others, atoned for that sin, and satisfied the wrath of God due it. What can a sinner do to be saved? The answer is nothing. We can do nothing to deserve God's favor or to merit His salvation. A Christian knows "that a man is not justified by the works of the law but by faith in Jesus Christ" (Gal. 2:16).

At issue, however, is more than knowing the right answer. What drove Isaiah and what drives Christians as ambassadors for Christ is a personal experience of the joy of sins forgiven and a reconciled relationship with the God they were created to glorify and enjoy. In other words, forgiveness is not merely a theological construct to be studied; it is a divine accomplishment to be savored and offered to others. Those who would speak of freedom from the debt of sin are themselves debtors to grace. The gospel is meant to be announced to all the world, to every generation.

We must stand at the fountain of God's forgiveness in the gospel before we can grasp its fruit and flow. The wonder of God's wisdom and glory of His grace that dealt with our sins will compel us in dispensing to others the grace we ourselves have received.

The Jewel of Justification

My wife has a ring that she inherited from her grandmother. The setting is remarkable, an ornate gold filigree with patterned white-gold banding. It shows real artisanship. But all that serves as preamble to the main attraction, a brilliant round diamond. A jeweler could no doubt describe the ring more accurately and vividly, but even a layman can appreciate its beauty.

When it comes to the ring Christ has given to His bride, the church, the centerpiece is the sparkling jewel of forgiveness. Like a diamond formed from carbon compressed in the earth's mantle, the demands of covenant law are met by the force of God's justice and cut magnificently to the contours of His righteousness. In the pledge of His troth, this God-designed, God-fashioned, God-bestowed gem of salvation is placed on our finger by His redeeming love, demonstrating that we belong to the One whose love will never waver or wane.

As the setting of a ring supports and directs attention to the stone at the center, so the jewel of forgiveness finds its setting in the doctrine of justification, what Martin Luther referred to as the article by which the church stands or falls. In Paul's unfolding of the gospel to the church at Rome, he makes the case that all are sinners, undeserving of God's affections and unable to remedy their own predicament. Against this backdrop, Paul opens the ring box of God's saving purpose to display the glory of the gospel and to extend that jewel of salvation to all who will receive it (see Rom. 10:9–13).

Paul spends much time in the first five chapters of his letter to the Romans talking about justification. Like that jeweler who could describe a setting with greater technical acumen and accuracy, Paul explains how justification works and how it supports forgiveness.

In question 33, the Westminster Shorter Catechism gives us a succinct summary of biblical teaching on the subject:

Q. What is justification?

A. Justification is an act of God's free grace, wherein he pardons all our sins, and accepts us as righteous in his sight, only for the righteousness of Christ imputed to us, and received by faith alone.

We can note several features. First, justification is an action, something that happens one time rather than progressively, like the signing of a marriage license. By grace through faith, a person is not being justified, but is *pronounced* justified, just like a couple is declared to be husband and wife and then lives out the realities of that union.

Second, justification is a pronouncement by God Himself, a legal declaration of guiltlessness and acceptance. The doctrine addresses two fundamental issues in respect to sinners before a holy God. On the one hand, it addresses the problem of sin. Our evil deeds are as filthy rags. But then even our best efforts are as filthy rags (see Isa. 64:6). Like smoke clings to everything in the wake of a house fire, the stench of sin infects even our most honorable of intentions. Nothing is untainted. In justification, God pardons the guilt of sin because Jesus atoned for that sin and redressed its guilt (see Isa. 53:6). To borrow another image, justification *cleanses* us from all unrighteousness.

The glory of the gospel is that though the wages of sin is death, "the gift of God is eternal life in Christ Jesus our Lord" (Rom. 6:23). As sinners saved by grace, our debt has not been merely waived, like we might waive the obligation of someone who borrowed money from us. Nor has it been pardoned, like a governor commuting the death sentence of a convicted criminal. In the case of a waiver or pardon, the guilt of sin remains, but its consequence is removed.

No, the gospel is the good news not that the debt of sin owed has been waived or pardoned but that it has been paid—in full. When it comes to the debt of sin before a holy God who must punish iniquity, we cannot pay it down through some sort of payment plan. We cannot negotiate a lesser obligation. We cannot escape through bankruptcy. Our debt must be paid, because God's divine justice must be satisfied. He would be less than holy, less than God, were He not to exact full recompense.

That is what the cross of Christ is all about. Jesus was born under law to redeem those under law. He came to pay the debt of sin. He gave His life as a ransom for many, a payment to satisfy the wages of sin owed. On the cross, He uttered words of legal transaction: "It is finished." The sense is that the debt is paid. The books are cleared for those He came to redeem, not by any trick of accounting but by payment in full for all sins past, present, and future.

The anthem of the believer is,

> My sin—O the bliss of this glorious thought!—
> My sin, not in part, but the whole,
> Is nailed to the cross and I bear it no more;
> Praise the Lord, praise the Lord, O my soul!"[4]

By grace, through faith in Christ, believers are debt-free, always and forever. God has provided no other means for the remission of sins, no other avenue for debt forgiveness. This

---

4. Horatio G. Spafford, "It Is Well with My Soul," public domain.

is why the Father holds up His Son in uniqueness, as *the* way, *the* truth, *the* life, apart from whom no one can be reconciled to Him (see John 14:6). The redemption offered by Christ is exclusive in that it stands as God's only appointed option. It is inclusive in that it is effectual to all who will believe: "All that the Father gives Me will come to Me, and the one who comes to Me I will by no means cast out" (John 6:37).

So on the one hand, the doctrine of justification addresses the problem of our sin. On the other hand, justification adorns us with a diamond of grace that shines with the luster of Christ's righteousness, His perfect obedience to the law of God. We are not left with a gaping hole where sin once stood. Rather, the flawless obedience of Jesus Christ is mounted in its setting for us to embrace and admire to the praise of His name.

Another portrait from the Old Testament helps us appreciate God's twofold provision in justification, dealing with both the guilt of sin and the gain of righteousness. The Israelites had returned to the Promised Land after exile for their covenant disobedience. The prophet Zechariah relates a vision of Joshua—not the Joshua of Jericho fame but the high priest of God. We see that Joshua has doffed his ornate vesture in exchange for brilliant white garments. In preparation for his annual duty in the inner sanctum of the tabernacle before the ark of God's presence, he was as pure as he could make himself, going through rituals of ceremonial cleansing and donning garments as spotlessly white as possible. Yet here is the assessment of the One before whom he stood: "Now Joshua was clothed with filthy garments" (Zech. 3:3). Filthy!

Before a holy God, Joshua's efforts at cleansing were for naught. An onlooker would see brilliant white brightness and splendor. But the God who knows the heart sees the stain. Just as with Isaiah, Joshua was unable to do anything to remedy his uncleanness. God acted. It is here that we find the two-pronged aspects of justification.

> Then [the LORD] answered and spoke to those who stood before Him, saying, "Take away the filthy garments from him." And to him He said, "See, I have removed your iniquity from you, and I will clothe you with rich robes."
>
> And I said, "Let them put a clean turban on his head."
>
> So they put a clean turban on his head, and they put the clothes on him. And the Angel of the LORD stood by. (Zech. 3:4–5)

Removal of sin's guilt and provision of clean garments— by God, by grace—anticipate the gospel of salvation. They point us to what God does and how He does it, through Yeshua, the greater Joshua who would bear the sins of others and clothe them with His righteousness.

Through this divine transaction our God expresses His faithful love, realized in the person and work of His Son. The jewel of His forgiveness forged by Christ is placed on our hand. Judgment is averted. Here we find another feature of our definition of justification. It comprises a divine transaction. It conveys a legal standing, a position achieved by God's grace and not by our merit or machinations. Christ's righteousness is imputed to us, credited to our account. By that transaction we escape condemnation and find acceptance.

But the Bible seems to give a mixed message. In one place we are told that all will face the judgment of God and His righteous scrutiny: "It is appointed for men to die once, but after this the judgment" (Heb. 9:27). But in another place, Jesus says emphatically: "Most assuredly, I say to you, he who hears My word and believes in Him who sent Me has everlasting life, and shall not come into judgment, but has passed from death into life" (John 5:24). How can that be? Will we face judgment or not? The answer is found in justification. By our own merit, we face condemnation. By faith in Christ's merit, we find commendation. And we can know that freedom from judgment not only at life's end but right now, in reconciled relationship with the living God. By faith in Christ, we have *already* come under judgment and been declared "not guilty," because He was found guilty in our stead. Saving faith puts all its eggs in that one basket of God's justification of the ungodly through Jesus Christ.

Gospel Breadth

The gospel communicates the forgiveness of sin, but it conveys more. It brings to the believer all the blessings of salvation, carried on the grace of God, propelled by His everlasting love. Jesus calls it "the gospel of the kingdom" (Matt. 4:23; 9:35; 24:14), expressive of glorious new realities bound up in Him as risen and reigning Lord. By the gospel, sinners once far off have been brought near by the blood of the Lamb and can astoundingly count themselves children of the living God, heirs of eternal life. They have been delivered from the kingdom of darkness and brought into the glorious kingdom of Jesus Christ, in whom they have redemption, the forgiveness of their sins. The gospel is God's comprehensive answer to a fallen creation, as far as the curse is found.

Yet in the display case of God's blessings, forgiveness is perhaps the trophy that stands most prominent. In the transmission of the news of the gospel, forgiveness is the headliner. The gospel provides God's answer to the conundrum of how sinners can be counted righteous in His sight. The gospel explains how a holy God can possibly justify the ungodly without compromising His character. That is why the gospel is so good and why it is news to be spoken to our flagging hearts and proclaimed to a needy world. We can note three basics about the relationship of forgiveness to the gospel.

Forgiveness is central to the gospel message. After His resurrection, Jesus interacted with two disciples on the road to Emmaus:

> Then He said to them, "These are the words which I spoke to you while I was still with you, that all things must be fulfilled which were written in the Law of Moses and the Prophets and the Psalms concerning Me." And He opened their understanding, that they might comprehend the Scriptures.
>
> Then He said to them, "Thus it is written, and thus it was necessary for the Christ to suffer and to rise from the dead the third day, and that repentance and remission of sins should be preached in His name to all nations, beginning at Jerusalem." (Luke 24:44–47)

This threefold division of Law, Prophets, and Psalms is short-hand for the whole of the old covenant Scriptures. Jesus was saying that the entire Old Testament had to do with Him. He summarizes the Old Testament's message with "It is written," a common expression for quoting Scripture. We would be at a loss, however, to find that quotation were we to scour the Hebrew canon, because it is the message of the *entire* Bible in a nutshell.

The Bible is a redemptive document that focuses on the person and work of God's Messiah. At the heart of that message is forgiveness of sin to be received not by reformation of one's ways but by repentance and faith in Jesus Christ as the Messiah of God.

Forgiveness is foundational to gospel promise. Peter testified about Jesus, "To Him all the prophets witness that, through His name, whoever believes in Him will receive remission of sins" (Acts 10:43). Again, we find reference to the Old Testament prophetic word. It is by faith in Christ that forgiveness of sin is found. Forgiveness achieved by Christ is extended to all who receive God's testimony and believe savingly on His Son. There is one salvation for Jew and Gentile, one name given under heaven by which any might be saved (Acts 2:21; 4:12).

Forgiveness is essential to gospel deliverance. The book of Acts describes the progress of the gospel message as it spreads from Jerusalem to Judea and Samaria, and to the ends of the earth—that is, to the Gentiles (see Acts 13:47). Paul, a major figure in the book, God's appointed apostle to the Gentiles, describes to King Agrippa the ministry given him by Jesus: "to open [the] eyes [of the Gentiles], in order to turn them from darkness to light, and from the power of Satan to God, that they may receive forgiveness of sins and an inheritance among those who are sanctified by faith in Me" (Acts 26:18). Forgiveness forms the first article of the declaration of independence for the believer who has been delivered from the kingdom of darkness and transferred into the kingdom of God's beloved Son. We declare this when we answer the first question in the Heidelberg Catechism:

Q. What is your only comfort in life and death?

A. That I am not my own, but belong with body and soul, both in life and in death, to my faithful Savior Jesus Christ. He has fully paid for all my sins with His precious blood, and has set me free from all the power of the devil. He also preserves me in such a way that without the will of my heavenly Father not a hair can fall from my head; indeed, all things must work together for my salvation. Therefore, by His Holy Spirit He also assures me of eternal life and makes me heartily willing and ready from now on to live for Him.

When Abraham Lincoln issued his Emancipation Proclamation on New Year's Day in 1863, shouts of joy echoed throughout the land as the news spread. To be sure, much hardship and struggle lay ahead, but the verdict was in. The slaves were legally free. With that declaration of deliverance came the promise of new life free from bondage and oppression. Such is the case with the gospel for all who believe in Christ alone for salvation.

The Joy of My Sins Forgiven

It was 1974. I was in my senior year of college and coming to grips with the gospel with which I had at best a nodding acquaintance. After all my years of involvement with organized religion, I knew the jargon, but I had no clue about the substance and certainly had no personal experience with it. Jesus was born in a stable. My response to that: "Merry Christmas! Let's trim the tree." When I would hear that Jesus died on the cross, I would think, "Okay. So what?" Jesus was raised from the dead. For me, that meant it was time to bring out the marshmallow chicks. Clearly, the significance of Christ's work was lost on me. I believed it happened but saw no personal relevance or importance in it.

There is a saying that if you don't have a pony in the race, the race will not be of interest to you. Talk of cancer will be merely academic until you are diagnosed with it yourself. The theological discussion of the gospel will remain at the level of the theoretical until a person comes to grips with how it applies to him or her. That is what happened to me in 1974. I learned I did have a pony in the race. I did have a terminal diagnosis. That was the first realization to my spiritually opened eyes.

Jesus said something intriguing yet puzzling. The religious leaders challenged Him about why He fraternized with sinners. In response Jesus answered, "Those who are well have no need of a physician, but those who are sick. I have not come to call the righteous, but sinners, to repentance" (Luke 5:31–32). At first blush it seems that Jesus is saying there were some who were not sick, some who were righteous and not in need of Him. But the point is not need. It is awareness of the need.

All of us are sinners, spiritually terminal, in desperate need of healing. God is the one who opens our eyes to that need and to His provision in Jesus Christ. The Westminster Shorter Catechism, question 31, captures well the biblical teaching:

> Q. What is effectual calling?
>
> A. Effectual calling is the work of God's Spirit, whereby, convincing us of our sin and misery, enlightening our minds in the knowledge of Christ, and renewing our wills, he doth persuade and enable us to embrace Jesus Christ, freely offered to us in the gospel.

That explains what happened to me. Because of the Spirit's work in my heart, the things I had heard before started becoming palatable, meaningful, and personal to me. I saw not just sin, but *my* sin. I saw not just the Savior, but *my* Savior, my hope of salvation, God's provision for my forgiveness.

From involvement with a Christian group on campus and attendance at an evangelical church, I began to learn things I had not in my previous two decades of exposure to the Bible, including the Bible's diagnosis, prognosis, and prescription. It was then, in late October 1974, persuaded and enabled, I retreated to my dorm room, knelt by my bed, and embraced Jesus Christ freely offered in the gospel. I experienced what Charles Wesley described:

> Long my imprisoned spirit lay
> Fast bound in sin and nature's night;

> Thine eye diffused a quick'ning ray;
> I woke, the dungeon flamed with light;
> My chains fell off, my heart was free;
> I rose, went forth and followed Thee.[5]

The starting point for an understanding of forgiveness is the personal experience of it through faith in Jesus Christ. We grasp our debt to love others by seeing ourselves as sinners undeservedly loved by God and as debtors to His amazing grace. If any of us would discover the healing properties of forgiveness in our relationships with others, we must first know the healing of our estranged relationship with God, the price at which that healing came, and what spurred such a great salvation.

A young woman stepped up to the microphone. The man in shackles had just been sentenced to forty years in prison for the murder of her father. Without rancor, she acknowledged the justice of that sentence, appropriate retribution for the atrocity of his crime. But she interjected, "At the same time, we are Christians, and as Christians we believe that Jesus loves you and forgives you. We hope that over time you will find the love of Jesus Christ in your life, and even in this terrible outcome, you will someday find redemption and protection in His mercy and love. We will be praying for you and your family."

We cannot help but applaud this young woman's stalwart faith and willingness to forgive. The beauty of the gospel shines for all to behold, to the glory of Jesus. But at the same

---

5. Charles Wesley, "And Can It Be That I Should Gain," public domain.

time, we must take exception to her understanding of how a person receives forgiveness. Christ's forgiveness cannot be received apart from receiving Christ. Forgiveness is not realized apart from faith. It would be more appropriate for the young woman to say that Jesus offers forgiveness and that her prayer is that her father's killer would find that forgiveness.

If we would find ourselves in a position to minister the grace of forgiveness to others, we must first have received that grace ourselves. Only then can we have an appreciation of what God has done for us in His Son so that we can respond in kind.

Not quite sure of my career goals, I pursued a master's degree in guidance and counseling at the University of Delaware. I was drawn to the field of counseling and figured the educational setting was as good as any to enter that field. I had come to Christ a few years earlier and read many books on the subject of Christian counseling, and by the time I entered the master's program, I had a well-developed biblical worldview. The program, however, was decidedly secular and contrasted markedly with the Bible's view of man and change.

Since I had a penchant for writing, I decided to write a book on the subject of counseling, contrasting the secular and biblical worldviews and helping me think through my philosophy of counseling. I wrote the book, had it typed up, and submitted it to publishers of the authors I had studied. Mercifully, God did not allow that book to see the light of day. It may have been a helpful exercise for my processing of things, but it was certainly not for public consumption. The problem was that even though I had researched the subject thoroughly, I had virtually zero experience and wrote without knowledge.

When it comes to readying ourselves to forgive others, simple study of the subject will not do. A true, compelling understanding of forgiveness cannot be merely academic. It must be experiential. Our heart must be gripped by God's astounding grace and awed at such a great salvation in reconciling us to Himself through the giving of His Son for us to be properly positioned to forgive others in like fashion. Only when we stand in Isaiah's sandals before a holy God to see the depths and vileness of our sin and have felt the profound and abject helplessness of our plight will we be inclined to forgive others as we have been forgiven.

Discovery Questions

1. What two needs do we have that God meets in justifying us?

2. How did He meet both of these needs in the gospel?

3. What is the relationship of justification to forgiveness?

4. How do the visions of Isaiah 6 and Zechariah 3 display the gospel?

5. Of all the blessings of salvation found in the gospel, in what way is forgiveness of sin most basic?

6. What are the various elements of justification spelled out in the Westminster Shorter Catechism, and how does each point us to God?

7. Did you discover the joy of your sins forgiven? If so, how?

Chapter 2
FORGIVENESS AS
KINGDOM CURRENCY

And forgive us our debts, as we forgive our debtors.
—MATTHEW 6:12

Bitcoins are becoming all the rage. I heard a story on the local news that a bitcoin ATM was just installed in the city of Philadelphia, one of thirty across the county. As I understand it, these ATMs do not allow for withdrawal. Rather, they allow only for purchase of bitcoins. That makes sense, I suppose, because bitcoins are digital currency. They exist only in a digital world. They are real but intangible.

Accompanying that story was the news that a real estate company was accepting this cybercurrency for purchase of certain condominiums. Depending on the bitcoin to dollar exchange rate, one of these units can be acquired for the asking price of B795, or $365,000. So bitcoins are unseen, but they have transactional value.

Just as the world of digital dealings has its own currency, so does the kingdom of God in a sense. Kingdom currency is vested with value at the cross of Calvary and is freely available for withdrawal to cover the debt of sin. That currency is forgiveness, and it becomes legal tender for relationship debt in kingdom dealings. In fact, we draw on that currency of grace daily in our relationship with God, and we deal in it in our relationships with others.

Jesus explains how forgiveness as a currency works in His parable of kingdom economics (Matt. 18:23–33). He describes a king owed a ridiculous sum by one of his servants. It would be like an American minimum-wage earner owing many millions of dollars. The king takes pity on the servant and liberates him from the debt. That same servant, however, encounters one who owes him money, a substantial amount but not exorbitant, something in the order of four months' wages. The second servant pleads for pity, but the first servant will have nothing of it. He orders the one in his debt to be ripped from family and home and remanded to the custody of the jailer until the debt is paid.

By this parable, Jesus is not commending the Golden Rule—"Do unto others as you would have them do unto you" (see Luke 6:31)—as much as He is describing how forgiveness is to function in the kingdom of God. We are to "pay it forward," dealing in the wealth of grace that we have received. The king's remarkable forgiveness of outrageous debt becomes the standard and point of reference for our forgiving others. That is why the spreadsheet of forgiveness is so extraordinary. It is not governed by customary banking practices but by the unreasonable accounting principles of grace.

We see this expressed in the model prayer Jesus taught His disciples to pray: "Forgive us our debts, as we forgive our debtors" (Matt. 6:12). Paul echoes the sentiment when he urged the followers of Christ to forgive one another. Even as Christ forgave them, they were to forgive (Col. 3:13). Christ gives us our mandate and our model for the forgiveness necessary to healing and health in relationships, as expressive of the gospel in which we have come to be partakers by the grace of God. Understanding forgiveness as redressing debt owed helps us to understand not only its freeing power but also how it functions for reconciliation.

Forgiveness Received

A woman had been married for twenty years. That union had produced three children. Husband and wife were able to buy a house and make a comfortable life for themselves through his full-time employment, her part-time work, and some reserves from an inheritance. But then the bottom fell out. The husband died unexpectedly. Financial reserves dried up. The debt that had been accruing for years started mounting up like accumulating snow in a blizzard. Even purchasing staples for subsistence became a challenge.

Compounding it all were the incessant letters and calls. Creditors swarmed like sharks to blood. Debt continued to pile up, new sources of money were found and then exhausted. The barely manageable blizzard became an avalanche of liability threatening life itself.

Then came the sheriff's sale. The widow returned home from her part-time job one day to find a notice attached to her front door indicating that the bank was foreclosing on her home and auctioning it off to satisfy her debt. No way out. She became frozen with fear. Her debt became enslaving and life defining.

The widow had no leverage, no power, no means, and no hope—until a benefactor stepped in with an offer to pay off all her bills and to cover any debt she would ever incur. No strings. No questions. No repayment, not that she ever could. Just freedom from the bondage of her debt. After a bout of skepticism, what would be the widow's reaction? Likely a relief she had not experienced in years would overtake her. Her heart would be awash with joy. The warmth of gratitude would spread throughout her being and ramp up with intensity the more she thought about it. One other byproduct of such generosity might be love—not romantic love but heartstrings of gratitude. That is the reaction Jesus highlights to Simon, a religious leader who took exception to Jesus for associating with sinners.

> And Jesus answered and said to him, "Simon, I have something to say to you."
>
> So he said, "Teacher, say it."
>
> "There was a certain creditor who had two debtors. One owed five hundred denarii, and the other fifty. And when they had nothing with which to repay, he freely forgave them both. Tell Me, therefore, which of them will love him more?"
>
> Simon answered and said, "I suppose the one whom he forgave more."
>
> And He said to him, "You have rightly judged." (Luke 7:40–43)

Although it may be true that money cannot buy happiness, dealing in the currency of kingdom exchange is a means to peace, joy, and love in the exercise of the grace of God.

The greater we see the debt of our sin forgiven, the greater will be our debt of gratitude and love to Him who lavished such grace on us. That gratitude increases as we grow in comprehension of the cost for such forgiveness. In fact, that growing realization of the wonder of God's forgiveness characterizes Christian maturity. When the Spirit initially opens our eyes to our sin and to God's remedy in Christ, we have a degree of appreciation. As we grow in our relationship with God, we discover that God is holier than we had conceived. In his vision, Isaiah the prophet was never more acutely aware of his sin than when he beheld the holiness of God. In the light of God's glory, we find our sin more heinous and extensive than we ever realized, meaning that the debt of that sin was more massive than we had ever grasped.

As of this writing, the federal debt of the United States is a little more than 19 trillion dollars. That's 19 with twelve zeros. We can hear that and understand that is a lot of money, but we can't really comprehend it. But the more we try to, the more incredulous we will grow. How much more when it comes to grasping the magnitude of the debt of our sin in light of the holiness of God!

But here is where our knees buckle in wonder and our hearts flood with love, gratitude, and awe. Where an audit of the debt of our sin exposes greater and greater liability to the justice of God's holiness, every invoice we find will be stamped "paid in full" at Calvary, where Jesus announced, "It is finished." This was a pronouncement that the debt of the sin He bore was paid—in fullness and finality.

As we continue to mature in the faith and see that chasm between a holy God and a sinful us widening, and the cross of Christ sufficient still, our love for God deepens and our gratitude for His mercies grows. This is the glory of the gospel, the potency of its saving power. The greater our sin, the more glorious God's grace. The apostle Paul expresses it this way: "But where sin abounded, grace abounded much more, so that as sin reigned in death, even so grace might reign through righteousness to eternal life through Jesus Christ our Lord" (Rom. 5:20–21). What an astounding bookkeeping measure! No matter how high the mountain of our debt of sin, it is dwarfed by the grace of God in Christ. Everest is eclipsed. What that means is that no matter where sin is found in our lives, at any point, to any degree, it has been accounted for by God and paid for by Christ. Thank you God!

I was explaining this dimension of the gospel to a class of prospective church members. I remember well Sandra blurting out, "That means I can sin all I want!" Sandra came from a background that emphasized the need for good behavior as the route to heaven. Her efforts at obedience to God's law were her matching contribution to Christ's redemptive work. For her, sin required that some personal atonement be made, to make up for the wrong done. In our class, we had explored that the formula of the gospel is not Jesus + my efforts = salvation. Rather, it is Jesus = salvation + my loving obedience. We had learned that no matching funds are required of us. In fact, our efforts to keep God's law merit us nothing. God's holiness would not allow for us to achieve a "good try" or to receive an *A* for effort. Rather, our efforts are like Confederate dollars offered to pay for goods purchased in Gettysburg. Salvation is bound up by Christ alone, offered by grace alone, and received through faith alone. You could see the wheels turning as Sandra came to grips with this gospel accounting, and that was when she said, "That means I can sin all I want!"

It was then I knew that she was starting to understand the gospel. In fact, her assertion is a natural one, even expected for a proper grasp of grace. That is why, after explaining a gospel that is nothing of our works but everything of Christ's, Paul anticipates the objection: "What shall we say then? Shall we continue in sin that grace may abound?" His answer: "Certainly not!" (Rom. 6:1–2). The apostle could not be more horrified or more emphatic. Our cleansing in Christ does not give us license to follow after sin. On the contrary, it demands we distance ourselves from it.

The good news of the gospel proclaims that we who have taken refuge in Christ stand forgiven of the entirety of our debt of sin—debt past, debt present, debt future. Jesus paid it all. All to Him we owe. That does not mean, however, that the blood of Christ bankrolls our sin. The very thought is abhorrent for God's holy children and an abomination to grace. To pray, "God, forgive me for what I am about to do" is foreign to gospel freedom. As Paul says, "And do not present your members as instruments of unrighteousness to sin, but present yourselves to God as being alive from the dead, and your members as instruments of righteousness to God. For sin shall not have dominion over you, for you are not under law but under grace" (Rom. 6:13–14).

Living Out the Riches of Forgiveness

We saw earlier that justification is an action of God's decree, a onetime verdict of "not guilty" in respect to the sins we commit and a once-for-all crediting of the perfect obedience of law keeping, both bound up in the work of Jesus Christ in our stead. He provides cleansing and clothing, atonement of sin, and allotment of an alien righteousness. All our sin has been accounted for and paid in full, forgiven finally, fully, and forever.

Even though our justification is a onetime declaration, however, it continues to have ongoing application. What part, then, does forgiveness play in our ongoing relationship with God? How does the positional forgiveness of justification relate to the progressive forgiveness experienced in sanctification, as we die to sin and live to righteousness? To put it in practical terms: Why must we ask God for forgiveness if we already stand completely and continually forgiven by Him?

In his first epistle, the apostle John helps us find our answers. Writing to believers, he emphatically states: "If we say that we have no sin, we deceive ourselves, and the truth is not in us" (1 John 1:8). Lest we think we misread, he says it again, this time making it personal with God: "If we say that we have not sinned, we make Him a liar, and His word is not in us" (1 John 1:10).

What is John talking about? He is saying that we as Christians continue to sin. If we think otherwise, we deceive ourselves. A realistic view of self in the mirror of God's Word will see the uncleanness of sin. John says nothing more surprising than what Paul does in Romans 7, where he relates his personal struggle with sin even after providing detailed reasoning that Christ had freed him from sin's guilt and power (Romans 3–6). All of us can relate to his admission:

For the good that I will to do, I do not do; but the evil I will not to do, that I practice. Now if I do what I will not to do, it is no longer I who do it, but sin that dwells in me.

I find then a law, that evil is present with me, the one who wills to do good. For I delight in the law of God according to the inward man. But I see another law in my members, warring against the law of my mind, and bringing me into captivity to the law of sin which is in my members. O wretched man that I am! Who will deliver me from this body of death? I thank God—through Jesus Christ our Lord! (Rom. 7:19–25)

Believers sin. It is part of our existence between here and glory. We are sinners saved by grace who are in constant need of Christ. We never go it alone. We never stand on our own. But as we become aware of our wretchedness, God has provided the method by which we find cleansing and peace, daily.

Once acknowledged, sin must be confessed. Sandwiched in between the bread of God's truth in 1 John 1:8 and 10 that we as Christians continue to sin is the meat of John's point that we must confess that sin: "If we confess our sins, He is faithful and just to forgive us our sins and to cleanse us from all unrighteousness" (1 John 1:9). These words both assure us and puzzle us, stirring in us both comfort and confusion. It is wonderful to know that forgiveness is ours for the asking. But why do we need to confess at all if our sin has already been forgiven?

To "confess" is to align ourselves with God. The word John uses, *homologeo*, literally means "to say" (*logeo*) the "same thing" (*homo*). To confess sin means we call our actions or inactions what God calls them. Not mere mistakes, not indiscretions, but sin—intentional or unintentional violations of the law of God. The psalmist puts confession in terms of acknowledging our transgressions:

> Blessed is he whose transgression is forgiven,
> Whose sin is covered.
> Blessed is the man to whom the LORD does not
>   impute iniquity,
> And in whose spirit there is no deceit....
>
> I acknowledged my sin to You,
> And my iniquity I have not hidden.
> I said, "I will confess my transgressions to the LORD,"
> And You forgave the iniquity of my sin. (Ps. 32:1–2, 5)

We uncover our sin, admitting it and refusing to hide it by rationalizations, blame shifting, or euphemism. We own up to our sin and we own our culpability. In turn, God covers it by no longer imputing iniquity, not reckoning debt.

This transaction of grace is founded on the assurance that God grants forgiveness. John tells us that when we confess our sin, God is "faithful and just to forgive us our sins." We can understand "faithful." God is true to His character and to His word. We wrap ourselves in the warm blanket of His abiding, unchanging love. The words of Paul that speak of assured blamelessness and certain preservation by God speak honey to our souls: "Now may the God of peace Himself sanctify you completely; and may your whole spirit, soul, and body be preserved blameless at the coming of our

Lord Jesus Christ. He who calls you is faithful, who also will do it" (1 Thess. 5:23–24). Because God is faithful, we will never find the cupboard bare or access denied.

We understand "faithful," but why "just"? We would have expected John to say faithful and *merciful* to forgive, not just. Mercy does not give us the consequence deserved. "Just," however, necessarily captures the transaction involved in forgiveness, how that forgiveness was achieved. The debt is paid. God's justice has been satisfied. Where and how was that done? At the cross. Ignoring the unhelpful chapter division at chapter 2 in 1 John,[1] that is exactly where John takes us: "My little children, these things I write to you, so that you may not sin. And if anyone sins, we have an Advocate with the Father, Jesus Christ the righteous. And He Himself is the propitiation for our sins, and not for ours only but also for the whole world" (1 John 2:1–2). Confession does not atone for sin, but draws on Him who did.

What that tells us is that *forgiveness is not found in mere confession of sin but in confession of Christ*, not in our admission but in His atonement. Jesus is our advocate, our defense attorney against the accusations of Satan. Satan points out our sin. Jesus counters that though the sin is real, He atoned for it. Our enemy the devil draws our attention to the abundance and heinousness of sin in our lives to drive us to despair. The Holy Spirit, however, convicts us of that sin to draw us to Christ.

---

1. While the Bible is inspired of God in the original languages down to the very singular and plural of words (e.g., Gal. 3:16), the chapter divisions and versification are not.

Jesus is the righteous One, the One who gave Himself, the Just for the unjust. He is the propitiation for our sins, the One who paid the penalty for them, the One who endured the wrath of God they deserved. In confession, we draw on the inexhaustible riches of God's grace, bound up in our justification. Justification is the gift that keeps on giving. Not that we accrue more righteousness, but we lay claim to what is ours in Christ.

John says that the blood of Christ "cleanses" us from all unrighteousness (1 John 1:9). The image of cleansing is attractive to us. It is like emerging from a smoke-filled room. The stench of sin clings to us. We feel dirty, unclean. To think that Jesus washes us, purifies us, and makes us clean sits well with us. But we don't want to stretch that metaphor too far. It is not as though in confession we pull ourselves up to the laver of Christ's blood as we would soiled hands to the bathroom sink, where we are not clean without washing. That would mean the dirt of sin's guilt is not forgiven without regular washing, so that if we were to miss a spot (that is, neglect to confess a sin), uncleanness would remain in God's sight. Rather, a better image is to think of sin as debt. Confession would be opening an accounts receivable ledger, looking up the debt of the sin we confess, and finding it has already been paid. We don't draw on Christ's blood to pay. We draw up to the ledger to discover it already paid by Him; the debt is wiped clean. God calls us to the throne of grace not to be forgiven but to find forgiveness.

Perhaps a better way to understand the forgiveness offered in 1 John 1:9 is to see it not as *receiving* forgiveness for sin confessed, but as *realizing* that forgiveness in greater

measure, like we would test the ability of something to withstand great weight. We note the scope of forgiveness in the
language John uses. If we confess our sins, God is faithful
and just to "cleanse us from all unrighteousness." We might
come before God with a particular sin in mind that we want
to confess. We find, though, that God cleanses us not only
from the guilt of *that* sin but from *all* unrighteousness. In
the confession of the one sin, we find forgiveness of all our
sins. This fits well with the idea that we are not so much
receiving forgiveness when we confess our sin but realizing
the forgiveness that has already been granted us by grace
through faith in Christ's atoning work. At the cross, all our
sin was accounted for—and paid for—in full.

Unbelievers cannot confess sin with the assurance that
they will be forgiven by virtue of their confession. Forgiveness is bound up in Christ alone. That is why John says Jesus
is the "propitiation for our sins, and not for ours only but
also for the whole world" (1 John 2:2). God has provided
no other way to pay the debt of sin and to escape its consequences than in the giving of His Son. He is the only way
of reconciliation for Jew or Gentile alike—the whole world.
Unbelievers can lay claim to the wealth of God's riches only
through faith in Christ.

The Unforgivable Sin

How is sin different for believers and unbelievers? In one
sense, sin is sin. It is rebellion against God, transgression of
His law, disobedience to His revealed will. The difference is
that for believers, sin is atoned for. Their guilt is removed.
The debt is paid. Unbelievers, however, remain saddled

with the guilt of their sin and continue to accrue debt that must be and will be settled at the judgment seat of God. Because they stand without Christ as their advocate, their sin is unforgivable. They have rejected God's only provision for sin's liability.

The religious leaders of Jesus's day asserted that Jesus was in league with the devil. He exposed the folly of such a notion and went on to say: "Assuredly, I say to you, all sins will be forgiven the sons of men, and whatever blasphemies they may utter; but he who blasphemes against the Holy Spirit never has forgiveness, but is subject to eternal condemnation" (Mark 3:28–29). What sin might this be? What offense could possibly be beyond the reach of Christ's blood?

Imagine you have been bitten by a rattlesnake. There is only one antidote. Thankfully, it is available and extended to you. You, however, refuse to avail yourself of that cure. As a result, you will die. The gospel writer employs that metaphor in explaining the availability and necessity of God's provision in Christ.

> And as Moses lifted up the serpent in the wilderness, even so must the Son of Man be lifted up, that whoever believes in Him should not perish but have eternal life. For God so loved the world that He gave His only begotten Son, that whoever believes in Him should not perish but have everlasting life. For God did not send His Son into the world to condemn the world, but that the world through Him might be saved. (John 3:14–17)

The reference to Moses recounts a time in the wilderness when people were bitten by poisonous snakes and faced certain death. God, however, instructed Moses to make a bronze snake and lift it up on a pole. All who looked to that remedy, presumably with faith in God's provision, would live. In the same way, all who look to God's Son lifted up on the cross to save would have life now and into eternity. They would not perish. Rather, they would have everlasting life. For those who rejected God's remedy, their affliction would remain and would take its course.

In effect, Jesus said, "He who blasphemes against the Holy Spirit never has forgiveness, but is subject to eternal condemnation." As Jesus would later explain in John's gospel, the role of the Holy Spirit is to bear witness to Him as the Savior of sinners, God's unique remedy. The unforgivable sin is to refuse to trust in Christ. It is not a matter of a transgression being beyond the scope of Christ's saving work. Rather, the unforgivable sin is not availing oneself of that saving work. Like ignoring the label on the antidote to a serpent's venom, denying the testimony of the Father and the Spirit (through His Word) to the efficacy of Christ's work leaves one without recourse to escape the judgment to come.

To reject the testimony of the Holy Spirit is to blaspheme God Himself who has given His Son and bears witness to Him. The unforgivable sin boils down to unbelief. That is why John goes on to say, "He who believes in Him is not condemned; but he who does not believe is condemned already, because he has not believed in the name of the only begotten Son of God" (John 3:18). John combines both diagnosis and prognosis at chapter's end: "He who believes in the Son has everlasting life; and he who does not believe the Son shall not see life, but the wrath of God abides on him" (John 3:36). By definition, believers cannot commit the unforgivable sin. God has worked faith in them by the regeneration of the Holy Spirit. We cannot invite unbelievers to confess their sin without confessing the Christ who is the end of sin.

But what happens in respect to our standing as believers before God when we do sin—as John has made it clear that we do? Our sin as believers affects our *fellowship* with God but not our *relationship*. When my children disobey me, I don't stop being their father. In fact, it is as their father that I deal with their sin in love. When we sin, we turn our backs on God to follow after sin, but God still loves us. John remarks on this love: "Behold what manner of love the Father has bestowed on us, that we should be called children of God!" (1 John 3:1). We can know ourselves as "beloved," called to love Him who first loved us.

That means we as believers confess our sins not as sinners to a judge but as children to a father. Confession does not return us to God's good grace but turns us to God's face, from which we turned to follow after sin. When we sin, we spurn God to run after something other than Him. We engage in idolatry, which is probably why John concludes his first epistle by insisting:

> We know that we are of God, and the whole world lies under the sway of the wicked one.
>
> And we know that the Son of God has come and has given us an understanding, that we may know

Him who is true; and we are in Him who is true, in His Son Jesus Christ. This is the true God and eternal life.

Little children, keep yourselves from idols. Amen. (1 John 5:19–21)

The journey of the Christian life is couched in terms of being true to Him who is true and who remains true to us, refraining from idols of the heart and seductions of the evil one.

Confession of sin should be part of our daily practice in walking with our God. In so doing, we draw on the inexhaustible riches of Christ in the forgiveness of our sin and refresh ourselves in the gospel. We renew ourselves in our standing in Christ. The well-known acronym ACTS (adoration, confession, thanksgiving, supplication) does well to keep confession as a reflection and requirement for gazing on the beauty of the holiness of our God.

But there's more that our God wants of us. He wants us to forgive *as we have been forgiven by Him*. As believers who have received forgiveness, He calls us to respond in kind. The God who has taken our hand and led us to the lofty vista of His amazing grace leads us down from the mountain to the uneven terrain of life with the motive and mandate to reciprocate.

Forgiveness Reciprocated

The Bible's teaching on giving helps us to understand God's desire and design for our forgiving others. In his first letter to Timothy, Paul charges him as a pastor to tell those who have wealth to recognize it as coming from the good hand of God and to "do good, that they be rich in good works, ready to give, willing to share" (1 Tim. 6:18). He approaches this principle from several different directions in his letter to the church at Corinth: "God is able to make all grace abound toward you, that you, always having all sufficiency in all things, may have an abundance for every good work" (2 Cor. 9:8). The upshot of it all is not only blessing to self and to others but glory to God: "You are enriched in everything for all liberality, which causes thanksgiving through us to God" (2 Cor. 9:11).

As what we have been given becomes a storehouse for sharing, so we minister to others the grace of forgiveness we have received. We apply the unseen kingdom currency of grace for the repair and rebuilding of broken relationships.

Forgiveness must be part of our outlook and agenda in relating to others as citizens of heaven and our disposition to others as kingdom ambassadors. The rhythm of discipleship is day by day. If we would follow Jesus, we must deny ourselves and take up our cross daily. The cross is an instrument of death, symbolic for us of putting to death our earthly desires and our seeking our own kingdom and glory above God's.

In the prayer that Jesus taught His disciples in the Sermon on the Mount (often called the Lord's Prayer but more aptly named the Disciples' Prayer), He instructed us to pray "Forgive us our debts, as we forgive our debtors" (Matt. 6:12). Just as we are to pray for our daily bread, so forgiveness of sin is part of our daily purview, in respect both to our own transgressions and to those who are in our debt because of their sin against us.

Earlier we recounted Jesus's story in which a servant is forgiven an enormous debt but in turn refuses to reciprocate by forgiving a much lesser debt owed him. Our Lord told this parable to show God's design for forgiveness, the expectation that we are to forgive as we have been forgiven. Such is the tenor of this demand that Jesus goes on to a bottom line that shocks us: "So My heavenly Father also will do to you if each of you, from his heart, does not forgive his brother his trespasses" (Matt. 18:35). We get it that we are to forgive others, but is Jesus informing us that the forgiveness we received can be rescinded if we don't? Can the debt of our sin be reinstated? To put it plainly, can we lose our salvation?

The introductory word "so" in Jesus's bottom line speaks not to logical consequence (e.g., therefore) but to example (e.g., in this manner). It is like playing ball with our children. We might say, "You kicked the ball, so I will kick the ball." We could either be saying that we will kick the ball *because* they did or we will kick it *like* they did. Jesus, here, is not issuing a threat but making a point. It is akin to His instruction in the prayer He teaches His disciples: "Forgive us our debts, as we forgive our debtors" (Matt. 6:12). He is laying out for us the reciprocity of forgiveness in kingdom exchange. We who have been forgiven much should always be prepared to forgive little. Any offense will be *little* compared to the mountain of debt forgiven us by our God. We might think it much, but that will only be because we have lost our bearings in the gospel of kingdom accounting practices.

Is there legitimacy in taking Jesus's statement as a reference to one's salvation? Is there an edge of warning in what Jesus says about God not forgiving us if we refuse forgiveness to others? In his commentary on the Lord's Prayer, Philip Ryken believes so. He says, "The ability to forgive is one of the surest signs of having been forgiven. It is proof that we have received God's grace. Those who are truly forgiven, truly forgive."[2] For Ryken, persistent unwillingness to forgive does not suggest that we can lose our salvation but that we perhaps never possessed it. Charles Spurgeon says the same thing in stark terms: "Unless you have forgiven others, you read your own death warrant when you repeat the Lord's Prayer."[3] So a person who fails to forgive others is not in danger of losing salvation but may be exhibiting a heart unacquainted with God's forgiveness in the gospel.

A word of caution is in order. We don't want to be presumptuous in declaring those who refuse to forgive to be unbelievers, but it is cause for circumspection. When we see in our own hearts hesitancy if not unwillingness to forgive those who sin against us, we see the need for a refresher course in the gospel. We want to take stock of the debt of our sin forgiven by God through the giving of His Son. It calls us to a different vantage point, seeing the log in our own eye before addressing the speck in another's.

Our Lord Jesus speaks of forgiveness from your heart (Matt. 18:35). A heart *awash* with awe of God's forgiveness, *accosted* by the unreasonable grace of God in its doing, and *aware* of its cost in the giving of His Son will be inclined

---

2. Philip Graham Ryken, *When You Pray* (Phillipsburg, N.J.: P&R, 2000), 138.

3. As quoted in Ryken, *When You Pray*, 137.

to operate on the principles of kingdom economics. Such a heart will forgive cheerfully and generously.

Exactly how do we apply these principles? What is forgiveness, and how do we practice it in dealing with those who have sinned against us—those in our debt? For that, we remove our academic garb and don overalls for the work required in the trenches of life's relationships.

Discovery Questions

1. How does the analogy of debt help us to understand the enslaving and liberating power of forgiveness?

2. Why do we need to confess our sins if they are already forgiven in Christ?

3. When you do confess your sins, what exactly are you doing?

4. What does John mean by saying that God is "faithful and just" to forgive our sins when we confess them?

5. What does it mean to say that forgiveness is not found in mere confession of sin but in confession of Christ (see 1 John 2:1–2)?

6. How might you deal with a reluctance in your heart to forgive someone who has wronged you?

7. Why must God's forgiveness of us be the point of reference for our forgiveness of others?

Chapter 3
PRACTICING FORGIVENESS

Forgiving one another, even as God in Christ forgave you.
—EPHESIANS 4:32

Jesus is our model for the Christian life. In Him we learn what it looks like to love God and neighbor. Peter holds up Jesus as our paradigm in suffering and relationship conflict:

> But when you do good and suffer, if you take it patiently, this is commendable before God. For to this you were called, because Christ also suffered for us, leaving us an example, that you should follow His steps:
> "Who committed no sin,
> Nor was deceit found in His mouth";
> who, when He was reviled, did not revile in return; when He suffered, He did not threaten, but committed Himself to Him who judges righteously. (1 Peter 2:20–23)

We can look at the way Jesus lived His life and find our example for how to conduct ours in His steps—but not when it comes to asking for forgiveness. Jesus teaches us about the need to ask forgiveness of others and stresses its importance and urgency. But He gives us no model. Why is that?

Recently, a major religious leader spoke on the account of a preteen Jesus going with His parents to celebrate the feast of the Passover in Jerusalem. At the conclusion of the time, His mother and Joseph set out for the return to Nazareth, but Jesus lingered behind in the temple to engage the teachers. Discovering Him missing, Jesus's frantic parents returned to Jerusalem and found Him in the temple. Mary couldn't believe her eyes. She asked Him, "Son, why have You done this to us? Look, Your father and I have sought You anxiously" (Luke 2:48). Jesus responded matter-of-factly, "Why did you seek Me? Did you not know that I must be about My Father's business?" (Luke 2:49).

The religious leader's comment was that Jesus likely had to ask forgiveness of His parents for what the leader called His "little escapade." We get from his remarks the idea that boys will be boys. Boys are unthoughtful and get into trouble, so they need to ask for forgiveness. The leader did note that the Bible does not say that Jesus asked for forgiveness or needed to ask for forgiveness, but that is something we can presume.

It may be that particular religious leader was speaking in social terms rather than theological terms, not saying that Jesus had sinned deliberately or inadvertently but that He would be polite and smooth things over with His anxious parents. He was sorry for inconveniencing them.

But this is not a topic to be trifled with. Nor should theologically charged terms like "forgiveness" be used so cavalierly, especially when it comes to Jesus. Scripture clearly says that Jesus was without sin. In speaking of the priestly work of Jesus, the writer of Hebrews makes the point that He "was in all points tempted as we are, yet without sin" (Heb. 4:15). The emphasis is that Jesus arrived at the cross of Calvary as a lamb without blemish, a sacrificial substitute without stain of sin. He had no sin of His own to pay the penalty for and was therefore qualified and capable to stand in the place of sinners. Paul spells out what is often called the great transaction: "For [God] made [Christ] who knew no sin to be sin for us, that we might become the righteousness of God in Him" (2 Cor. 5:21). For that transaction to be possible, Jesus had to have no sin debt of His own.

In no way could Jesus have asked for forgiveness of His parents for any lack of love or disobedience on His part. We can find no example, explicit or implied, of Him asking for forgiveness or needing to ask for forgiveness. However, we do find clear instruction from Him on how we are to practice forgiveness, both in asking it of others and in granting it to them. We can begin by exploring the terms Scripture uses.

The Meaning of Forgiveness

We want to grasp first what forgiveness is before we can explore how to go about its practice. Two Greek words help us in understanding the dynamics of forgiveness. The first word (in order of address, not importance) is *aphiemi*. This is the term used by our Lord in Matthew 6:12 in the Disciples' Prayer, in which we ask our Father in heaven to forgive our debts as we forgive our debtors. It is also the word Peter uses when he asks Jesus, "Lord, how often shall my brother sin against me, and I forgive him?" (Matt. 18:21).

The thrust of this term is to let go, dismiss, or drop. When someone sins against us, it is like we are given a promissory note of debt, payable on demand. To dismiss it is to tear it up. If someone lashes out at me in anger, spewing insults and hurtful speech, that person is in my debt. I have a hold over him because he has wronged me. When I forgive, I let loose that hold. I drop the ammunition I had against him. It is no longer available to me as a weapon. I am not just to holster the weapon; I must discard it.

The other word translated "forgive" in the Greek New Testament is *charizomai*. We find this term at the core of Paul's charter of Christian unity: "Therefore, as the elect of God, holy and beloved, put on tender mercies, kindness, humility, meekness, longsuffering; bearing with one another, and forgiving one another, if anyone has a complaint against another; even as Christ forgave you, so you also must do. But above all these things put on love, which is the bond of perfection" (Col. 3:12–14).

This word puts a positive spin on forgiveness. Its root is *charis*, grace. Grace is something that is unearned, undeserved, and unexpected. In forgiving, we give grace—freely. We let the offense go not because the offender deserves it, but as an act of grace. We forgive as we have been forgiven. We forgive in the model Jesus calls for in His parable of the unforgiving servant (Matt. 18:22–33, which uses *aphiemi*), looking first to the extravagant grace we have received. Our action is driven not by just desert but by the exercise of gracious generosity. We cancel the debt as an act of willful love.

What instruction do these terms give us in the threat of conflict or heat of battle? Let's say a husband and wife are arguing. It has gotten pretty intense. Each spouse has reached deep in their gunnysack of hoarded offenses looking for ammunition against the other. God's wisdom would be to drop the matter before the fight erupts. We will learn about preemptive forgiveness in a bit, but this couple has not chosen that route. They have engaged in battle and taken up arms.

The counsel of *aphiemi* would be "drop the weapon and back away." It may be that one spouse has a hold on the other, one of those "You always do this" statements, or "That's just like you." Perhaps example is piled on example, like blow after blow, trying to pummel the other into submission—and win. But *aphiemi* disarms itself.

The counsel of *charizomai* takes a more positive, proactive approach. It looks to disarm the other by graciousness, putting into practice the proverb, "A soft answer turns away wrath, but a harsh word stirs up anger" (Prov. 15:1). It may take the tack of admitting wrong and owning up to one's contribution to the conflict. *Charizomai* may see the fault in the other but choose not to give it the weight of blame that could be given, instead responding with grace and sensitivity.

We see this approach outlined by the apostle Paul in regard to the tongue: "Let no corrupt word proceed out of your mouth, but what is good for necessary edification, that it may impart grace to the hearers" (Eph. 4:29). This approach calls for caution and control but also empowers to bring help and healing. The goal is not to win but to win over for the goal of Christ. It exercises the propensity of forgiveness for being a peacemaker.

These two terms frame the starting point, the posture for the exercise of forgiveness. Whenever someone approaches us to ask for our forgiveness, we want to harken to the debt of our own sin so graciously forgiven us. The only way we can get our bearings for undertaking *aphiemi* and *charizomai* is to reflect on God's grace to us in canceling the debt of our sin, including the ransom He paid to do so, and His remarkable conveyance of compassion. Without those bearings, we will lose our way and be puffed up in pride. We will think ourselves other than the sinners saved by grace that we are and so lose the posture necessary to stand against the true enemy's divisive efforts.

The Path of Forgiveness

Now, having grasped what forgiveness is, how do we go about dispensing it? We can boil it down to two actions. Let me mention at the outset that these actions are neither perfunctory nor easy. Sometimes when we are given steps to follow, the process and the outcome can seem rather automatic, like mixing the right ingredients in the proper manner will certainly yield the desired cake. But the path of forgiveness is an arduous one, often filled with thickets and hazards. We need to have our wits about us. It cannot be mindless and certainly not heartless. In fact, our Father works at the level of our hearts to make us more proficient as the peacemakers He calls us to be. He does this in the arena of conflict.

It is probably my imagination, but it seems that pastors I know experience a greater degree of hurt and rejection than people in other professions. Maybe that is because the pastoral role involves being a lightning rod for the strikes of others. I know I, as a pastor, have learned the necessity of being grounded in Christ—just as a lightning rod must be grounded—that the brunt might fall on Him rather than me and I might not be scorched by others' criticisms. In my own experience, some have made the effort years later to acknowledge sin against me and to ask for my forgiveness. I'm sure I have wronged others in the way I have handled things, and I believe I am open to the Spirit's conviction in my heart. There are times of betrayal when those closest to me have hurt me deeply. I have employed the principles of forgiveness that I will share in a moment, but I know well how hard it is to carry them out. It is so easy to keep a record of wrongs. It is easy to allow embers of bitterness to smolder within, ready to erupt in flame and to engulf the heart. Even with destroying all physical reminders, the engrams of memory are amazing vessels of storage, often kept in a manner that exonerates me of any wrong and enshrines the wrongs of others in distilled and distasteful form. It is an insidious business. God's grace is assuredly sufficient for both my heart and my following the path of forgiveness, but that grace meets opposition of pride that needs constant attention. Forgiveness in its giving and receiving involves humble reliance on God. Keeping that in mind, let's move to the steps we take on the path of forgiveness.

Remove
First, to forgive is to no longer hold the offense against the person who sinned against us. Remembering that God is

our model (we forgive *as God forgave us*), we want to follow His lead.

My wife and teenage son and I were sitting at the dinner table catching up on our days. Linda had made a delicious meal of pulled pork. As we ate and talked, Nathan got a piece of the pulled pork on his cheek. He was relating something in conversation that was pretty serious. Linda and I were intent on giving him the attention that the issue deserved. I looked over at my wife and saw her trying her best not to break the seriousness of the moment by laughing. Finally, we couldn't hold it any longer. We had to tell Nathan about the rogue piece of pork so he could remove it and we could pay attention to what he was saying.

That is the way it works when someone sins against us. We have trouble looking at them without seeing their sin. In forgiving us, God removes our sin from us as far as the east is from the west (Ps. 103:12). How far is that, east from west? They are polar opposites. The person and the sin are put at contrary ends. To look at one is not to look at the other.

When we forgive, we disassociate the sin from the person. The piece of pulled pork is not only taken off, it is taken out of sight. Growing up where I did, we did not have trash pickup. We would have to bag the garbage up and cart it to the dump. There we would toss it in the pile and leave it behind. That is what we need to do with an offense when we forgive others. We remove it from them and we remove it from our sight, putting it where it belongs as refuse.

In Isaiah 38:17 we are told that God casts all our sins behind His back. Of course, God is spirit and has no back or body. But He speaks in these anthropomorphic terms to accommodate Himself to our understanding. How well can you see something behind your back? You can't, and that is precisely the point. It is out of sight, no longer associated with the person—by virtue of the act of forgiveness.

How do we maintain that position of disassociation? So often, we remove an offense but want to carry it at the ready in that gunnysack or keep it in a drawer to retrieve when we want advantage. In fact, we may well have a drawerful of such transgressions, neatly organized by offense like so many pairs of socks. But genuine forgiveness owns no such drawer. Genuine forgiveness is not granted a concealed-carry permit. The weapon is tossed. The offense is jettisoned. That leads us to the other action involved in forgiving.

Remember Not

The first step on the path to granting forgiveness is to no longer hold the offense against the person who sinned against us. The other shoe to forgiveness, the second action in this walk of love, is to remember the sin no more. In the first place, we separate the offense from the person, removing it from him or her. In the second we purpose not to remember it any longer. Remove and not remember are the steps we follow on the path of forgiving someone.

Notice I did not say to *forget* the sin. "Forgive and forget" is not a biblical concept. It sounds good and appropriate on the surface, but it presents us with an untenable demand. It is one thing for a jury to be instructed to disregard testimony in its deliberations. It is quite another for them not to be tainted by it. We can't unring a bell. The language of Scripture is better expressed not as forgive and forget, but as forgive and not remember. We can't flick a switch and forget, but we can work at not remembering.

As we've seen, God is our exemplar in the practice of forgiveness. Notice how His forgiveness is expressed:

> I, even I, am He who blots out your
> transgressions for My own sake;
> And I will not remember your sins. (Isa. 43:25;
> cf. Jer. 31:34).

How do we go about not remembering? Not remembering works on the principle that whatever we don't feed will die. When I was growing up, the field behind my house was filled with poison ivy. I played in that field. I could handle the poison ivy with my bare hands and be unaffected by it. Evidently, I was not allergic. Fast-forward thirty years. I am married with kids, living in a home with a yard to care for. I noticed poison ivy growing around a row of tall pine trees on my property, the vines starting to make their way up a couple of trees. No problem. I went out one Saturday and pulled the offending plants off the trees and out of the ground with my bare hands. It wasn't long after that that raised red patches erupted on my arms—very itchy red patches. Apparently, previous experience was not an accurate indicator of present encounter. Either that or I had developed an allergy or perhaps was playing with fire by pushing things too far. But here is what I discovered. If I scratched the itch, it got inflamed and itched more. If I resisted and ignored the cries of the itch, it settled down and healed. After a while, it healed and stopped its incessant nagging for attention.

That is how we work at not remembering—by not scratching. We feed it no more by no longer bringing it up. We go about this disremembering in three ways.

First, we no longer bring it up to the *person* we forgave. After all, didn't we forgive them? Isn't the guilt of their offense no longer available to us? Didn't we cast it in the rubbish heap rather than store it in a drawer? This sort of forgiveness is an exercise of love. Love "keeps no record of wrongs," as the New International Version puts it (1 Cor. 13:5). The ledger is tidy. No balance is maintained to carry over to another billing cycle. Accosting those who have wronged us with an offense for which we have "forgiven" them makes *us* the ones sinning against them.

Two men were talking. One told the other that every time his wife and he argued, she got historical. The other man said, "Don't you mean hysterical?"

The first guy responded, "No, I mean historical. She brings up everything I ever did wrong."

That is funny in a joke, but not in real life. We sin by dusting off all the offenses we were supposed to have jettisoned when we forgave the other person.

Second, in disremembering we no longer bring it up to *others*. That is called gossip, and it is insidiously destructive. It burns as a wildfire, enflaming our hearts, singeing other relationships. The writer of Proverbs cautions us: "He who covers a transgression seeks love, but he who repeats a matter separates friends" (Prov. 17:9; see also Prov. 26:20).

Gossip can be tricky. It can be like those stinkbugs that find their way into our homes and we can't figure out how they got in. One way for gossip to slip in is hidden in the vehicle of prayer requests. "Please pray for my husband, who stumbled in drunk the other night." That is nothing less than sin masquerading as an angel of light. We can be quite creative when it comes to finding ways to repeat a matter, but the result is the same. It separates close friends, and it keeps the matter alive to exert its damaging influence.

Third, we no longer bring it up to *ourselves*. Like that itch that begs for our attention, we must refuse to scratch. We do not allow it audience in our minds, though it clamor for attention. We follow the counsel of Paul, who instructs us in what should occupy our thoughts: "Finally, brethren, whatever things are true, whatever things are noble, whatever things are just, whatever things are pure, whatever things are lovely, whatever things are of good report, if there is any virtue and if there is anything praiseworthy—meditate on these things" (Phil. 4:8). Rather than think destructive thoughts, we want to fill our minds with constructive thoughts. In fact, replacing the blameworthy with the praiseworthy is one method for permanent expulsion of the old, akin to evicting bad tenants and leasing the apartment out to good ones. Plus, the benefit of meditating on the praiseworthy is realized, like a healthy diet to physical fitness. The thrust is not so much positive thinking as it is profitable thinking, thinking that edifies and contributes to the goal of peace. We want to take every thought captive to the obedience of Christ (2 Cor. 10:5).

Through these three aspects—not bringing the offense up to the person, to others, or to ourselves—we work at not remembering (see chart below). By God's grace, over time the force of the offense will weaken and perhaps even die.

STEPS ON THE PATH TO FORGIVENESS

"…as God in Christ forgave you." (Eph. 4:32)

Remove the offense (Ps. 103:12; Isa. 38:17)
Remember it no more (Isa. 43:25)
    Offender (1 Cor. 13:5)
    Others (Prov. 17:9)
    Ourselves (Phil. 4:8)

We had to put my dachshund of fourteen years to sleep. I had the job of taking him to the vet. I don't want to get into too much detail or I'll rile the emotions I experienced then. Rather than have the vet dispose of the body, my wife wanted the dog buried in our backyard. My son dug the hole and put the cardboard box in and filled it back up with dirt. He chose to move a good-sized rock that would serve as a marker on top of the grave.

I have mixed feelings about that marker because it provides a reminder. I see it when I mow the lawn back that way, and I think of Oscar. But when we forgive, we don't want a marker. We don't want old feelings stirred up, old memories resurfaced. We want to drop the offense in the grave, cover it with love, and leave it buried, with no grave marker to remind us of it. That might mean even getting rid of items in our possession that we associate with the offense, if possible. Perhaps it will be forgotten, but at the very least it will be recognized as dead, a fitting image for an offense we have forgiven.

DIY Forgiveness

Asking for forgiveness typically involves some sort of exchange. It is transactional. We see that with God. 1 John 1 invites us to take the initiative to confess our sin to God, admitting it, acknowledging it as a violation of His revealed will, and categorizing it as wrong. In so doing, God in His faithfulness and justice grants us forgiveness for that sin. The offense is removed, fellowship restored. A transaction has occurred. We have listened to God's assessment of our action and heeded His invitation to the mercy seat. In turn, God hears and bestows assurance of pardon and abundance of grace, both rooted in the saving work of His Son on our behalf.

We see a similar transaction in the psalmist's exchange with the covenant God:

> I acknowledged my sin to You,
> And my iniquity I have not hidden.
> I said, "I will confess my transgressions to the
> LORD."

The psalmist affirms God's response: "And You forgave the iniquity of my sin" (Ps. 32:5). The psalmist's uncovering of his sin is met with a declaration of God's mercy and grace in forgiveness.

Transgression of one person against another is also best handled by way of transaction. Jesus describes two situations of offense, one in which a person is sinned against, the other in which a person has sinned against another. As our Lord describes them, both situations recognize fault, involve interaction—personal contact of some sort—and include transaction. Attempt at eliciting a response is made:

> Therefore if you bring your gift to the altar, and
> there remember that your brother has something
> against you, leave your gift there before the altar,
> and go your way. First be reconciled to your brother,
> and then come and offer your gift. (Matt. 5:23–24)

> Moreover if your brother sins against you, go and tell
> him his fault between you and him alone. If he hears
> you, you have gained your brother. (Matt. 18:15)

The best way to deal with an offense is face-to-face or, if necessary, voice-to-voice. That allows for the personal dimension and the give-and-take of talking it through and working it out together. Personal presence is helpful. It is hard to hug over Skype or over the phone. A personal letter can be useful in some instances, particularly in giving more reasoned explanation if that is warranted, provided that the explanation does not rationalize wrong. But it is always best to interact personally to conduct the transaction of requesting and extending forgiveness. I have discovered that the worst way to deal with relationship problems is through e-mail. There is no opportunity to gauge tone. Even a smattering of emoticons won't help. Often e-mails exacerbate matters, because innocuous comments can be construed negatively by the recipient and so complicate matters. The upshot is that the conflict can become more entangled and combustible. Personal contact that allows for give-and-take, nonverbal expression, and power of presence is much preferred for constructive communication.

So, ordinarily, personal interaction is preferable for the transaction of forgiveness. But what about those times when the person who sinned against us doesn't ask for forgiveness? Ideally, when one has sinned against another the two will meet in the middle, on their way to seeking reconciliation. Our Lord starts each out on the path in Matthew 5:24 and 18:15, with the command to "go." If you sin against a brother, you go. If a brother sins against you, you go. However, there are those times we will not make mountains out of molehills or refrain from addressing a wrong for what we perceive a greater good. In those instances we exercise the discretion of *unilateral* forgiveness.

Our Bible's concordance will be of no help in finding the expression "unilateral forgiveness," although there are passages where it is intimated (e.g., Mark 11:25). Rather, it is inherent in the rule of love for the healing and preservation of relationships. When Paul instructs God's children to "be kind to one another, tenderhearted, forgiving one another, even as God in Christ forgave you" (Eph. 4:32), he is saying we need to maintain a disposition of love. We operate in the spirit of forgiveness. The grace of God flows from an orientation of our hearts, and it zeroes in on our responsibility. As Paul put it to the Romans, "If it is possible, as much as depends on you, live peaceably with all men" (Rom. 12:18). Our involvement in thought and deed contributes to our being a peacemaker, not a troublemaker; part of the solution, not part of the problem.

We might call this DIY forgiveness. Anyone who has been to Home Depot or Lowe's knows what DIY is—*D*o *I*t *Y*ourself. We find the material and tools at these big box stores and undertake the project ourselves, perhaps under the tutelage of a YouTube video. We can call this exercise of forgiveness DIY not because we do things in our own strength or wisdom, but because we do not have opportunity or make occasion for the transactional exchange of forgiveness, so we take what measures we can into our own hands.

Proverbs 10:12 gives us guidance in such forgiveness: "Hatred stirs up strife, but love covers all sins." "To cover" (*kasah*) is to destroy or overpower, to hide and keep hidden. The psalmist extols the blessing of covered sin, not that it is hidden by denial, but that it is no longer available for accusation:

> Blessed is he whose transgression is forgiven,
> Whose sin is covered.
> Blessed is the man to whom the LORD does not
>   impute iniquity,
> And in whose spirit there is no deceit. (Ps. 32:1–2)

We cover the sin of those who sin against us by the application of forgiveness in the exercise of love. We overlook an offense (Prov. 19:11; see also Prov. 17:14). We unilaterally purpose not to hold it against the offender any longer and to work at not remembering. Without opportunity to transact, we ourselves act. We take up the toolbox of love, stocked with patience, kindness, compassion, forgiveness, and other biblical implements, and go by ourselves to the offense and set to work on it through the healing measures of the gospel.

Unilateral forgiveness exercises real forgiveness. It unilaterally applies the two steps in the process of forgiveness as an expression of love in those times when we deem the situation warrants. Its deficiency lies in that it does not confront the offender's sin, and it does not accomplish reconciliation that could be pursued by transaction. We do want to note, however, that just as David prepared the materials for the temple that Solomon would build, unilateral forgiveness does deal with issues of our own hearts (like bitterness and anger) and paves the way for transaction should our God provide occasion. In addition, if our heart finds no rest or our conscience continues to accuse us, it may be that we will need to make special effort to address the matter with our brother, if possible.

The Goal of Forgiveness

It was a bitter cold January morning. Heavy drops of rain fell on the freezing ground and created a thin layer of ice everywhere they touched. Walking was treacherous. But by noon the temperature had risen into the low forties. I headed out my front door, arms filled with bins of plastic and glass and bags stuffed with newspapers to put out for recycling. In my brisk pace, my foot found a patch of ice with water on top of it. I went flying in the air one way, the recycling another. I came down with my full weight on the edge of a step. I immediately knew something bad had happened.

It turned out that bad thing was a partially torn quadriceps tendon. Surgery was not required, but slow convalescence and steady rehabilitation were. Over the months, I graduated from a series of braces that first protected the area from further harm and then allowed for increasing movement, and eventually strengthening. My goal, though, was not healing of my quad. My goal was to once again walk up the stairs two at a time, to return to normal functioning, to get back on the tennis court. In other words, my aim was not merely recuperation, it was restoration.

That is how it works with the healing of forgiveness, which can also take time. Forgiveness is not the goal; it is a step toward the goal. Like removing a splinter and cleaning out the wound, forgiveness sets the stage for healing and rebuilding. That rebuilding involves dealing with sin in our own hearts and perhaps in the lives of those we have forgiven. It entails reestablishing some degree of relationship that, as far as it depends on us, honors Jesus Christ.

In a sense, to grant forgiveness is to conduct a business transaction centered on the debt of someone's sin against us. For that reason, we may not feel like forgiving them, but we purpose to do it. Just like love in Scripture can be commanded, so can forgiveness. It is something we can act on in obedience and grow in in dependence on Christ, through whom we can do all things. That includes loving the person we cannot possibly imagine loving.

Some will say to forgive without feeling like it is hypocritical. However, just like we might not feel like getting out of bed in the morning to go to work but do so anyway because we know we should, we can forgive as an expression of love to God and neighbor. We can apply the balm of Gilead as an ointment of grace to the strained and bruised relationship.

Forgiveness takes work. It cannot be flippant or perfunctory. It involves more than forcing our children to begrudgingly say "sorry" when they commit an offense against a playmate. It must be from the heart (Matt. 18:35), which takes work and begins with a heart inclined toward

God. The heart is where we plant the seed that by God's grace will blossom into a thing of beauty. Forgiveness gives destructive weeds like bitterness and resentment no room to grow, no opportunity to flourish.

As was mentioned at the outset of this chapter, forgiveness, whether in the granting or the receiving, is not as simple as it might seem when it is reduced to steps to take. Even though it was more than twenty years ago, Bill's being molested by an uncle when he was twelve continues to haunt him. Like a locale that still bears the marks of a tornado from long ago, the inner terrain of his psyche bears the scars of his experience. He has healed, at least in some measure, but like a dormant virus, his guilt and pain erupt at the slightest provocation. When Bill gave his life to Christ, he brought that guilt and shame to Him. Bill experienced a peace he had not known before. He forgave his uncle, and that lifted a weight from him and opened his horizon to the green pastures of freedom. Grace bathed his soul, wiping away the guilt and restoring his soul. But, like that latent virus, guilt would flare up and need to be subdued once again in the power of the gospel. The grace of forgiveness is something we need to be ready to apply as needed, bringing to bear the sufficiency of Christ even as we take up our cross daily. We have an enemy who would wrest us from the security of our Savior's arms and rob us of the peace bound up in Him.

If forgiveness is an integral part of the Christian's journey, given us by God for the welfare of the body and exhibition of God's new society, and if our sufficiency is in

Christ, then it is in Christ that we must abide.[1] The writer of Hebrews points us to Christ:

> Therefore we also, since we are surrounded by so great a cloud of witnesses, let us lay aside every weight, and the sin which so easily ensnares us, and let us run with endurance the race that is set before us, looking unto Jesus, the author and finisher of our faith, who for the joy that was set before Him endured the cross, despising the shame, and has sat down at the right hand of the throne of God. (Heb. 12:1–2)

As we fix our gaze on Jesus, we behold three things to help us on our way. *Christ is our example.* We are to forgive as we have been forgiven. Forgiveness is neither easy nor cheap. It comes at great cost and requires great purpose. We might not suffer the cost of our life, but we humble ourselves at expense to ourselves. *Christ is our strength.* We are to find our ability in Him. Only by abiding in Him can we root out spiritual cancer, find healing, and be instruments of healing. Our endurance is found in His suffering and sufficiency. *Christ is our Lord.* We are to follow His desire for our lives and not our own. Our feelings and preferences are real, but they cannot rule the day. The throne on which He is seated with kingdom authority is one that we have bowed before

---

1. Only by abiding in Christ will we produce the fruit of Christian character. Jesus insists that apart from Him we can do nothing. In Him, however, we can do all things that He requires. For explanation and application, see Stanley D. Gale, *A Vine-Ripened Life: Spiritual Fruitfulness through Abiding in Christ* (Grand Rapids: Reformation Heritage Books, 2014).

in worship and allegiance. These are the sorts of things of which we remind ourselves as we cultivate a forgiving spirit in our hearts, in running the race set before us, a race that involves relationships. We've seen the basics of practicing forgiveness, but Scripture brings us more areas to consider in going about it. It is to these we turn our attention in the next chapter.

Discovery Questions

1. How do the two words translated "forgive" help us to understand how to go about it?

2. What challenges of heart do you encounter in pursuing forgiveness?

3. What two steps direct you along the path of forgiveness?

4. If someone has wronged you, what three ways can you undertake to forgive and not remember?

5. What is the difference between transactional forgiveness and unilateral forgiveness?

6. In what ways is forgiveness a pivot point rather than an end point for a relationship?

7. What dangers are there in allowing sin to fester in your relationship with God, with others, and in your own heart (see Heb. 12:14–15)?

Chapter 4
AUTHENTIC FORGIVENESS

If your brother…repents, forgive him.

—LUKE 17:3

It was my first day of seminary. A friend and I were embarking on our studies at Westminster Theological Seminary in Philadelphia. We headed out from Newark, Delaware, for the ninety-minute commute, something we would do five days a week for the next four years. We knew the route, having traveled it in our visits to the seminary. It was fairly direct, mostly on major roads. About an hour into the trip we arrived at the entrance to the Pennsylvania Turnpike, the last major leg of the journey. To our consternation, the turnpike was closed. Evidently, there had been a major accident that had shut all eastbound lanes. We had to adjust our plan, but we knew no other route to take. This was in the day before GPS and when gas stations gave out free folding maps. We secured a map and eventually made it to campus. That experience certainly made us appreciative of the smooth sailing we would have every day from then on.

That is the way it works with forgiveness. We can have it all mapped out and have clear guidance on how to go about it, but there will be issues that invariably arise along the way. In travels, it can be traffic accidents, blocked roads, or wrong turns. When it comes to the practice of forgiveness, other factors and considerations can rise up to challenge us. This chapter addresses some of those.

Faux Forgiveness

We are surrounded by fakes. Cell-phone towers made up to look like trees. Building façades that make dull masonry look like elegant stone. In watching a movie, it can be impossible to distinguish the real from the computer generated. These efforts are not intended to deceive but to delight. Approximation to reality is close enough.

The same can be true of forgiveness. People can express sorrow appropriately for any number of things. "I'm sorry for getting back to you so late." "I'm sorry for the inconvenience in giving you the wrong information." "I'm sorry to hear about the death of your father." But being sorry for a wrong you have done falls short of the demands of forgiveness. A sharp disagreement erupted between two women. Through direct and indirect comments, the conflict escalated. Finally, after weeks of avoiding each other, they talked. They didn't talk through the issues and grievances. They didn't identify their own contributions to the conflict. Rather, they faced off and offered a weak "I'm sorry" to the other.

These women had acknowledged a rupture in their relationship and nodded in the direction of some sort of wrong each had done. They felt the weight of Christian duty. But mouthing the words "I'm sorry" is a pale shadow of asking for forgiveness. Like a child saying "because" in answer to why he did something, saying "sorry" is only the prelude to the matter, the entrance to the freeway. Though the road to forgiveness has been entered, it has not yet been traveled. At best, sorrow for conflict or a wrong done sets the stage for healing; at worst, it puts a bandage over a festering sore.

Another deficient candidate to the grace of forgiveness is apologizing. Apologizing involves public expression of something amiss that you were involved in and sorrow for negative consequences resulting from it. It appears to have more substance than saying "I'm sorry," in that it is offered as an overture of reconciliation and not just regret. Sorry speaks to something inside us. To some extent, an apology can engage the other person and may even elicit a response ("That's okay."). But apologizing *requires* no response of the one wronged, nor does it seek it. It is like throwing a ball to someone without concern for its being caught. But to say, "Will you forgive me?" puts the ball in their court and involves them in the reconciliation process. It makes demands of them. Apologizing acts to dismiss a grievance. Forgiveness engages the other and sets out on a course of peace, together addressing an offense.

The 2016 Olympics in Rio experienced more than its share of problems. From green pool water to unfinished venues to polluted rivers to transportation issues, the problems were in the news as much as the athletic events. In *USA Today*, writer Josh Peter went so far as to say, "If apologizing were a medal sport, Rio Olympics spokesman Mario Andrada would be vying for the gold." At each day's press briefing, Mr. Andrada would issue an apology for one thing or another.

While apologies can be helpful in recognizing wrong and fostering a climate of conciliation, they don't necessarily bring with them a plan of action. That's particularly true in a ruptured relationship. Apologizing sets the stage for personal engagement, but it does not require it. Apologizing can be an end. Asking forgiveness is a beginning.

Even worse is the faux apology, a favorite in political circles, the pyrite of precious metals: "I want to apologize to anyone who might have been offended." Again, it involves public expression of something amiss, something affecting others, and regret for negative consequences resulting from it. But what is missing is acknowledgment of wrong done. It is almost like apologizing for calling someone ugly by saying, "I'm sorry you're ugly." There is no ownership of the deed, no acceptance of responsibility, and contrition only for the consequence—not personal conduct.

A husband and wife were experiencing public adversity. News of their situation was rampant on social media, created headlines for many months, and evoked all sorts of public sympathy. The husband had been wrongfully imprisoned for his faith, away from his wife and homeland. In a surprising revelation, the wife acknowledged that their marriage was not what it seemed to be and claimed she had suffered all kinds of verbal abuse from her husband. She asked the public for forgiveness. Her sin? Not letting the public know sooner what a cad her husband was. Her confession ended up being a litany of charges against her husband.

Forgiveness was the card laid on the table. But it was nothing more than a joker that had no business being part of the deck. We must be careful in dealing with forgiveness, whether in the asking or the granting, that it conform to the biblical definition. The term "forgiveness" can be freely bandied about, but closer examination shows that it bears no resemblance to the biblical description and does great violence to the gospel and even the biblical worldview. Just because something has shared characteristics with forgiveness does not mean it will stand up to scrutiny and function as God intends, any more than a cheap knockoff of a luxury watch will measure up to the real thing. Faux forgiveness can do more harm than good.

Forgiveness and Repentance

Just as being sorry and apologizing are inadequate expressions of asking for forgiveness, so the forgiveness requested may be inauthentic. Imagine the unthinkable, at least for an eight-year-old. She unwraps a Tootsie Roll Pop—cherry, her favorite kind. She savors it as the candy shell gets smaller and smaller. Finally, she gets to the center only to find there is no Tootsie Roll. The question is, is it still a Tootsie Roll Pop without the Tootsie Roll center? The wrapping may be authentic. The shape is expected. The taste and texture both conform. But a key element, perhaps *the* key element, is missing—the candy core.

When it comes to asking for forgiveness, does a core of repentance need to be evident or at least present at some point for the forgiveness to be genuine and received as such? This chapter opened with the words of Jesus: "If your brother...repents, forgive him." Does a request for forgiveness need to be wrapped in words that express sorrow, regret, and contrition that reflect a heart of repentance? Is forgiveness without repentance just empty words? To take it a step further, are we relieved of our responsibility to forgive when we don't discern a degree of repentance? Even more sobering, in granting forgiveness to someone who is not repentant, do we in some way become an enabler of that person's sin by not recognizing it or dealing with it? After all, the issue is not merely our broken relationship. The concern is primarily about God and the holiness He desires and the unity in truth He wants. Even though David had sinned against Bathsheba by committing adultery with her; against her husband, Uriah, by having him murdered; and against the entire nation of Israel by acting as a selfish shepherd, in his confession in Psalm 51:4 he said,

> Against You, You only, have I sinned,
> And done this evil in Your sight—
> That You may be found just when You speak,
> And blameless when You judge.

Sin is first and foremost against God. When we grant forgiveness, must we be sure that the offender is truly repentant so that God is honored, sin is recognized, the real issue is dealt with, and the design of God for sin's redress is maintained (see Matt. 18:15–17)?

For example, if Joan were to ask Barb to forgive her for criticizing her in front of their friends, should Barb expect to hear an expression of repentance or probe to see if Joan was really contrite for what she did? Is there some sort of prescreening where we are called to discern regret before we grant the forgiveness asked of us? Is it wrong to forgive someone who expresses no authentic, or at least acceptable, sorrow for her wrong?

This touches on our discussion of DIY forgiveness. If repentance is a prerequisite for granting forgiveness, does that mean unilateral forgiveness is unwarranted and ill-advised because it does not attempt to discern or demand repentance? Does it do more harm than good by possibly letting sin fester unaddressed? Is it actually unloving, like not drawing someone's attention to an imminent danger would be? After all, sin left unchecked can become more entrenched and poison hearts and relationships.

Two passages help us to find our bearings in addressing the necessity of discerning a core of repentance for granting forgiveness. The first is recorded in Luke's gospel account and gives the larger context for what we quoted above. It makes explicit reference to the presence of repentance in the transaction of confession and repentance:

> Take heed to yourselves. If your brother sins against you, rebuke him; and if he repents, forgive him. And if he sins against you seven times in a day, and seven times in a day returns to you, saying, "I repent," you shall forgive him." (Luke 17:3–4)

The second passage is recorded by Matthew and arises from Peter's trying to pin Jesus down on one's duty to forgive.

> Then Peter came to Him and said, "Lord, how often shall my brother sin against me, and I forgive him? Up to seven times?"

> Jesus said to him, "I do not say to you, up to seven times, but up to seventy times seven." (Matt. 18:21–22)

In Matthew's case, Jesus does not reference repentance, but that could be because He is not addressing the question of quality, but quantity. Both passages, however, speak to the responsibility to grant forgiveness for multiple offenses.

Our Lord Jesus stresses several things. First, if our brother expresses repentance, we are *commanded* to forgive the offense. Jesus does not say that we are to forgive only when our brother repents, but that when our brother does repent, we are to forgive. It may be that our Lord is simply using the word "repent" as synonymous with asking for forgiveness or owning up to sin, something like a mother telling her son, "I want you to wash the sink" and then reminding him, "I told you to scrub the sink." Different ways of saying the same thing.

We could diagram our Lord's direction this way:

If your brother sins against you → rebuke him.
If your brother repents [of sin against you] → forgive him.

Notice the parallel. The sin of the brother is replaced with a change, a new stance. The former posture is antagonistic. A grievance has intruded on the relationship, necessitating rebuke. The latter posture is sympathetic, where the offending brother has changed direction and is now moving toward the person sinned against. By granting forgiveness, the offended one receives his brother. The focus is on our stance to our brother for his good and for healing in the relationship. The Lord emphasizes *our* responsibility in the situation: "Take heed to yourselves" (Luke 17:3). As far as it concerns us, we are to be at peace. We are not to remain hardened or standoffish.

Or Jesus could be saying that repentance must be present for forgiveness to be accomplished. A person who forgives an offense without hearing words of regret or contrition that reflect a heart of repentance could be minimizing sin and dressing up the division cosmetically, like putting makeup on a bruise rather than addressing the root issue. The problem with understanding a demand for repentance is in what Jesus goes on to say: "And if he sins against you seven times in a day, and seven times in a day returns to you, saying, 'I repent,' you shall forgive him" (Luke 17:4).

This redirects the discussion from what is a genuine expression of forgiveness to what is a genuine expression of repentance. Three terms are found in the New Testament that contribute to an understanding of genuine repentance. They involve (1) godly sorrow, (2) a reorientation of mind, and (3) a change of direction. We can see how these terms create a flow: sorrow leading to change of mind leading to change of behavior. Godly sorrow has to do with grief over the harm to another, as opposed to a worldly sorrow that is concerned only for consequences to self. It represents a grief over sin that originates from and is motivated by a concern for God (see 2 Cor. 7:10–11). From that point of reference, repentance will adopt a change of mind. The Greek term is literally expressed "against the mind" (*metanoeo*). This is the word Jesus uses for repent in Luke's passage. From that new opinion will come actions that reflect the new orientation, as Paul described his mission to King Agrippa: "that they should repent, turn to God, and do works befitting repentance" (Acts 26:20). If I repent of leaving my dirty clothes on the floor, the fruit of putting my dirty clothes in the hamper will result from my repentance.

Herein is the problem. If we are commanded to forgive someone who repents seven times a day, how can we know the repentance is genuine? Indeed, blatant serial offenses (seven times in one day!) would suggest the repentance is not genuine. True repentance will result in the fruit, the out-working, of a reversal of mind in changed behavior. But, as we've seen, serial forgiveness does not allow time to examine the fruit of serial repentance in order to test its genuineness. We are not afforded the opportunity to run a credit check to approve redressing the current debt. Yet we are commanded to forgive.

John worked with his brother Bill in a real estate office. John had to be away on a particular date and would not be available to oversee the closing on a house he had sold, so he asked Bill if he could step in and see things through. Bill agreed. The problem was that Bill forgot all about it and did not show up for the settlement. When John found out, he was livid and took Bill to task for it. After the initial explosion, when John settled down to the point they could actually talk to one another, Bill admitted his wrong and asked John to forgive him. John said he could not. His reason? Bill had not sufficiently exhibited the fruit of repentance.

Jesus said that if a brother sins against you seven times in a day and returns to you asking for forgiveness (or "repents"), it is required that you forgive that brother. Does John have biblical ground for not forgiving Bill? Does the mettle of Bill's repentance need to be tested for genuineness? If so, what would such fruit look like in quantity and quality, and by what standard?

Though Jesus expresses asking for forgiveness in terms of repentance, does He do so as a qualification for granting forgiveness (Is the forgiveness authentic?), or is He simply describing someone wanting to make amends? In other words, the act of asking for forgiveness implies a wrong committed and an indebtedness that needs to be settled. The asking itself is a fruit, albeit in seed form, an overture of conciliation, a change of direction from away to toward. Is waiting to see if that seed germinates and produces change resulting from genuine contrition and good intention necessary for the granting of forgiveness, or is Jesus saying that no matter the number of offenses, we should be open to reconciliation? When Jesus tells us we must forgive an offending brother seven times in a day, He suggests that an incubation period for repentance is not warranted for granting forgiveness, and should not be insisted on as such.

What this means is that when Bill asks John to forgive him for his dereliction, particularly a dereliction he has owned up to and regrets, it is incumbent on John to forgive and begin the work that forgiveness entails. If John is reticent, he must take stock of his own heart with the help of the Holy Spirit to try to understand his reservation. It may be that John will come to the conclusion that he simply does not want to forgive his brother, in which case the command of Christ and character of the gospel need to be brought to bear. Or, it could be that John recognizes his reticence, and it will be a matter of submission in doing as the Lord insists and asking the Spirit to reveal his heart and soften it with the irrigation of living water.

As we observed in His interaction with Peter, our Lord does not mention repentance. In fact, He doesn't even speak to the transaction of asking for forgiveness. It may be that by "seven times in a day" (Luke 17:4) or "seventy times seven" (Matt. 18:22), Jesus is not so much laying out the mechanics or requirements for the transaction of forgiveness or speaking to the authenticity of the forgiveness asked as He is displaying the nature of grace in the model of God. In other words, Jesus is not highlighting repentance, but showcasing an extravagant grace to the extent that the disciples protest their faith is insufficient for the task: "And the apostles said to the Lord, 'Increase our faith'" (Luke 17:5). They recognized how hard it would be to forgive and their need for divine assistance. This emphasis on unreasonable faith versus overt repentance is reminiscent of the passage we alluded to earlier from Mark's gospel where Jesus said, "And whenever you stand praying, if you have anything against anyone, forgive him, that your Father in heaven may also forgive you your trespasses" (11:25). Here forgiveness is granted without transaction and without expression of repentance and is expressive of a faith that moves mountains (Mark 11:22–23), including a rock of offense, in dependence on Christ.

The rule of love inclines us to forgiveness (see Col. 3:12–14). As we are irritated at a pebble in a shoe, love is not at ease with division. It needs to be dealt with. Forgiveness, or at least its active ingredients, is the means to address that division and promote healing. It may be the issue will need to be pursued through the reclaiming process Jesus outlines in Matthew 18, but a love armed with forgiveness will be the catalyst.

Where does this lead us? Are we to look for a profession of repentance when someone asks for forgiveness of sin against us? We are, but not because Jesus uses the word "repent." We don't need to hear the magic words "I'm sorry" or "I have sinned" to obey Christ's command to forgive. Rather, we want to see contrition borne out of concern for the character of sin that has invaded the relationship to wreak its divisive havoc. Whether we have been party to willful sin or inadvertent consequence, sin's effects are to be lamented. Grief over sinning against another is a healthy sign of grace and the conviction of the Holy Spirit, something we long to see in ourselves and in our brother. Most of all, we want to see sorrow for wrongs motivated by concern for the glory of God who hates sin, the honor of Christ who wants unity, and recognition of the root issue of division in the healing power of the gospel. Movement by an offending brother against the one offended is laudable and to be welcomed, and by God's grace will result in a sober dealing with sin and healing in the relationship.

Forgiveness is decidedly Christian, reflecting the One most grievously sinned against. Only by the grace of God bound up in Jesus Christ can we approximate such forgiveness. We shake our heads to hear Jesus's answer to Peter, "seventy times seven." We can hear ourselves protesting. "You mean, when they do the same thing?" "Shouldn't I wait to see if they change, if they really meant it?" "Wouldn't it be wise to make them squirm a bit? After all, they need to know how much they hurt me, or at least how wrong they were." Seventy times seven—unreasonable grace.

What Forgiveness Doesn't Do

I've never quite understood statutes of limitation. If a crime has been committed, how can its prosecution have a shot clock? Perhaps it has to do with the credibility of witnesses after a certain time or the ability to construct a viable case with evidentiary value. Right now, states around the country are reexamining their statutes of limitation for sexual crimes. Prosecutors are frustrated by having their hands tied with decades-old evidence coming to light. The public is outraged over the injustice of it all and is raising its collective voice to prompt change to extend the legal expiration date stamped on certain offenses.

Forgiveness is not like that. While it deals with the guilt of an offense, it does not remove concern for the offender or promote sin by allowing it to run rampant. Forgiveness does not permit a dog known to be violent off its leash to inflict further harm, even though it may waive the consequences of an attack.

God has great concern for the sin in our lives and what that sin can do to relationships. By His grace and wisdom in the cross, He has provided remedy for the guilt of that sin. He has given direction for the exercise of forgiveness in the healing of relationships. But God has also given vast counsel in His Word that we might deal with sin that remains and experience the healing power of the gospel. The New Testament Epistles speak to what new life in Christ looks like, both personally and in relationship. For example, Peter offers a template for rebuilding after the removal of toxicity by the exercise of forgiveness:

> Finally, all of you be of one mind, having compassion for one another; love as brothers, be tenderhearted, be courteous; not returning evil for evil or reviling for reviling, but on the contrary blessing, knowing that you were called to this, that you may inherit a blessing. For
>
> "He who would love life
> And see good days,
> Let him refrain his tongue from evil,
> And his lips from speaking deceit.
> Let him turn away from evil and do good;
> Let him seek peace and pursue it.
> For the eyes of the LORD are on the righteous,
> And His ears are open to their prayers;
> But the face of the LORD is against those who
>   do evil." (1 Peter 3:8–12)

God does not countenance continued evil. Rather, He wants sin dealt with. While we may strive to not remember in the practice of forgiving, that does not mean we become unaffected by the offense or unconcerned about the continuing influence of a person's sinning. Immunity for prosecution in dropping an offense does not mean losing the opportunity to address sin.

To the Colossians, Paul describes love as the overgarment of forgiveness: "But above all these things put on love, which is the bond of perfection" (Col. 3:14). Love covers over, but it is not a cover up. It is not dismissive of sin. It neither excuses sin nor is an enabler to sin. It is correct to say that we forgive someone's sin, but it is more precise to say that we absolve the guilt of the sin. We forgive the debt incurred by the sin. We remove its offense. However, there may well remain consequences, ramifications, and repercussions with which we must deal. A criminal may find forgiveness from the one against whom he committed a crime but may still face a penalty and still have to make restitution. A person caught in a sin may be freed but at the same time may require another to pull alongside him to bear his burdens (see Gal. 6:1–5).

Granting forgiveness does not mean that efforts at resolution or reconciliation are lost to us because we removed the offense and must work at not remembering it. To accomplish the rebuilding, restorative goals of forgiveness, we may need to bring the offense to the table. The difference is that the offense is now brought forward for healing rather than for harm. Figuratively speaking, instead of the parties being separated by the offense on the table, they convene on the same side of the table, working together to deal with it. They are allied against a mutual foe, that the evil one might not find a foothold (Eph. 4:27).

When someone sins against us multiple times and we forgive that person using the formula of seventy times seven, though we have set aside the guilt, we may have to deal with issues of the heart and practices in their lives. In addition, granting forgiveness does not guarantee instant trust. Keeping no record of wrongs neither induces a naivety nor ignores tendencies. If someone has stolen from us, we are likely to keep our eyes peeled. Jesus was not ignorant about what was in people's hearts, and neither should we be.

When we forgive, we are to put on love. Jesus commands us to love even our enemies. That doesn't mean we are called to generate a rosy, warm feeling toward them or become best buddies. But it does mean we seek our God for a godly attitude and a relationship that honors Him. We take up the mantle of peacemaker laid out for us in Romans 12:14–21:

> Bless those who persecute you; bless and do not curse. Rejoice with those who rejoice, and weep with those who weep. Be of the same mind toward one another. Do not set your mind on high things, but associate with the humble. Do not be wise in your own opinion.
>
> Repay no one evil for evil. Have regard for good things in the sight of all men. If it is possible, as much as depends on you, live peaceably with all men. Beloved, do not avenge yourselves, but rather give place to wrath; for it is written, "Vengeance is Mine, I will repay," says the Lord. Therefore
>
> "If your enemy is hungry, feed him;
> If he is thirsty, give him a drink;
> For in so doing you will heap coals of fire on
>   his head."
>
> Do not be overcome by evil, but overcome evil
>   with good.

In this passage love is expressed in practical terms designed to treat fellow sinners as image bearers of God rather than as objects of our disdain (see Luke 6:27–36). Scripture holds out for us a minimum comportment for our treatment of others, even though we may never recover any level of intimacy with them. The salient features found in forgiveness empower us as peacemakers in the healing power of the gospel.

Forgive and Never Forget

Following the conquest of the Promised Land under the leadership of Joshua, the Reubenites, Gadites, and the half tribe of Manasseh set out to return to their land on the east of the Jordan River. Before they crossed the Jordan, however, they paused to build an altar of imposing size.

Hearing that, the nine and a half tribes that remained in the land of Canaan mobilized for war. They gathered themselves before the two and a half tribes and accused them of treason against the Lord their God. The trans-Jordanian tribes responded with great vehemence that they were doing no such thing. Rather, they had erected the altar not for sacrifice but as a remembrance that they, too, were part of the people of Israel. Once the memories of war had faded, they did not want the descendants on either side to think that the natural boundary of the Jordan River suggested a division among the people of God.

They laid out their reasoning:

Therefore we said that it will be, when they say this to us or to our generations in time to come, that we may say, "Here is the replica of the altar of the LORD which our fathers made, though not for burnt offerings nor for sacrifices; but it is a witness between you and us." Far be it from us that we should rebel against the LORD, and turn from following the LORD this day, to build an altar for burnt offerings, for grain offerings, or for sacrifices, besides the altar of the LORD our God which is before His tabernacle." (Josh. 22:28–29)

These tribes reflected God's desire for unity among His people. All sorts of boundaries and barriers can impose themselves to threaten that unity. The trans-Jordanian tribes erected an altar by the Jordan River, what they thought could be a barrier that would speak against unity.

In like fashion, our Lord has given us an altar not of sacrifice, but of remembrance. It harkens to the true altar on which sacrifice was made, the cross of Calvary that held the Lamb of God who takes away the sin of the world. In the Upper Room, before He went out into the night to be betrayed by sinful men, Jesus expressed His heart in prayer:

> I do not pray for these alone, but also for those who will believe in Me through their word; that they all may be one, as You, Father, are in Me, and I in You; that they also may be one in Us, that the world may believe that You sent Me. And the glory which You gave Me I have given them, that they may be one just as We are one: I in them, and You in Me; that they may be made perfect in one, and that the world may know that You have sent Me, and have loved them as You have loved Me. (John 17:20–23)

Jesus's desire was for His saving work in the gospel to bring healing and to showcase that peace in relationship with brothers and sisters in Christ, for the world to take notice.

This altar of remembrance is the Communion table, around which is celebrated the Lord's Supper. Those who partake of the elements remember His death until He returns not as a sacrifice for sin once again, but to claim those for whom He died. Those assembled commune together with their risen, reigning, returning Lord. They point to His atoning death for the remission of their sin and proclaim unity among those of kindred faith. "The cup of blessing which we bless, is it not the communion of the blood of Christ? The bread which we break, is it not the communion of the body of Christ? For we, though many, are one bread and one body; for we all partake of that one bread" (1 Cor. 10:16–17).

This "altar" stands as a constant remembrance of where our forgiveness is found and of the need to forgive as we have been forgiven, in reminder that we are one body. Every time we celebrate the sacrament, we hear the voice of our Lord: "Is there an offense you are holding onto against a brother or sister in Christ? Are you refusing to forgive the puddle of sin against you, even though I forgave the ocean of your sin against Me? Let it go. If you can't, then go, with haste. Leave the offerings you brought. Be reconciled to your brother. Then come and worship Me, the God of peace."

Discovery Questions

1. How are saying "sorry" and apologizing different from asking for forgiveness?

2. What impostors to forgiveness have you encountered? How do they differ from biblical teaching?

3. Why is an expression of repentance desirable for the conduct of forgiveness (see Luke 17:3–6)?

4. What is the relationship of Christian love to forgiveness (see Col. 3:12–14)?

5. Why does granting forgiveness not tie our hands for helping someone in habitual sin?

6. How does Romans 12:14–21 instruct us in our responsibility to be peacemakers?

7. In what ways does the sacrament of the Lord's Supper highlight unity among God's people and showcase how it is achieved and maintained?

Chapter 5
WHAT ABOUT FORGIVING OURSELVES?

...to open their eyes, in order to turn them
from darkness to light,
and from the power of Satan to God,
that they may receive forgiveness of sins
and an inheritance among those who are
sanctified by faith in Me.

—ACTS 26:18

A car careens into a tree because the alcohol-impaired driver fails to negotiate the curve on the road. His wife of five years is killed when her side of the vehicle makes direct impact. Their infant daughter, strapped in the backseat, survives but suffers injuries she will carry with her for the rest of her life.

That incident haunts the man, a follower of Christ who took a wrong turn. He has confessed his sin to God and believes that he has found forgiveness. He has even received forgiveness from his in-laws. But he cannot forgive himself, knowing that his actions brought such pain to others. Therefore, the forgiveness from God and his in-laws never seems to find home in his heart, held at bay by this inability to forgive himself, barring him from the peace he so desperately wants.

He has sought professional counseling. As much as it hurts to relive the moment, he finds it a help to express his grief. Perhaps somehow he will discover a way to assuage his guilt and move on. But like a leaky basement in a downpour, no sooner does he leave the office than he finds his heart filling up with self-blame once again. In trying to deal with it all, he hears repeatedly how much more difficult it is for people to forgive themselves than it is to forgive others. He can attest to that.

But what are we to make of the concept of forgiving ourselves? There is something appealing, even necessary, about it as we pursue the peace that eludes us. When we commit an offense against another person, when our fault plays prominently in some sort of tragedy, we naturally blame ourselves. The weight of guilt can be oppressive, even unbearable. Self-forgiveness seems the logical route to finding freedom from the oppression of self-blame. After all, have we not tasted the power of forgiveness to deal with guilt and remove blame in our relationships with God and our fellow man? Surely, it is appropriate for us to bring that remedy to bear through forgiving ourselves.

But is that God's way? Is there another transaction to be undertaken for grasping the healing power of the gospel? Along with forgiveness gained from God and those we wronged, is forgiving ourselves a leg in our race to peace? As some suggest, is self-forgiveness even foundational to forgiving others, something we must first address if we would fully realize the forgiveness we receive by God and others we have wronged?

A Sweeping Forgiveness

Certainly God is in the business of forgiveness. We have spent time exploring the beauty and design of remission of sin found in the gospel. As an expression of His love, through forgiveness God provides relief from the scourge of sin and crippling weight of guilt. We have witnessed the amazing healing power of the gospel that reconciled us as sinners to a holy God, and we have seen the need to administer that comfort to others with the comfort we ourselves have received. Spread across the pages of Scripture, with old covenant anticipation blossoming into new covenant realization, the cost of forgiveness is seen in sacrifice. Through *the* sacrifice of the cross, the sinned-against God mercifully and graciously gave His only Son to be the sin bearer, the unique means for forgiveness of sin and freedom from guilt.

The message of forgiveness echoes throughout the Scriptures, both in terms of personal relationship with God and in terms of relationships among God's people. Jesus brings both facets to bear in the model prayer He taught His disciples: "Forgive us our debts, as we forgive our debtors" (Matt. 6:12). His parable of the unforgiving servant (Matt. 18:21–35) illustrates the lavish grace of God in forgiving offenses against Him and compels our forgiving in like fashion others who sin against us.

Paul admonishes those in Christ to forgive others. Standing at the heart of the charter of Christian unity he says, "Forgiving one another…; even as Christ forgave you, so you also must do" (Col. 3:13). Forgiveness seems to be part of the DNA of Christian love, where we are to be ready to drop a grievance against another in the exercise of the grace we have received.

The sun of God's forgiveness shines gloriously in the Bible, dawning as it does in the fullness of time with the coming of Jesus Christ to deal with sin. The call for us to forgive others rises like the harvest moon, reflecting the warmth and brilliance of that sun of forgiveness we have received in Christ. The landscape of redemption is beautiful for it.

The story of the Bible is a tale of forgiveness, promised in the garden of Eden, procured at the cross of Calvary, and proclaimed in the gospel. It speaks both of knowing the joy of our sins forgiven through trust in Christ and also of our forgiving others who wrong us.

But the Bible never speaks of forgiving ourselves. Not a word. Not a whisper. Not a hint. A document replete with teaching on forgiveness is silent, either by instruction or illustration, on the subject of forgiving ourselves.

What do we make of that? Is a sense of guilt and shame something new to the human experience, unknown to the saints of old? Has modern psychology unearthed something unaccounted for by God? It certainly seems appropriate to turn to self-forgiveness as a means of stepping outside the shadow of guilt that obscures the light and warmth of God's love, even as an application of the forgiveness of the gospel. But what does God say?

A Broken World

When we visit the doctor's office with a complaint, our physician will not only have us describe our symptoms but will also explore how they started. What happened to bring about the current condition? Likewise, taking stock of the onset of sin and shame proves helpful for us in understanding the condition of our heart and its susceptibilities. Our first insight into guilt comes to us from the opening pages of the book of Genesis. The first two chapters of the Bible introduce us to an eternal God and describe His creating work. Genesis 2:25 closes the account of God's handiwork by noting that our first parents were "naked…and were not ashamed."

Nakedness has to do with more than being unclothed. It speaks to an openness, a vulnerability without fear of exploitation or mistreatment. The first couple was exposed without shame and experienced not just absence of embarrassment but lack of disgrace or indignity. That is a beautiful picture of marriage, where a man and a woman can be completely exposed to one another—physically, yes, but also emotionally, intellectually, and spiritually—and not experience shame from the other. I present this picture when I prepare couples for marriage and try to show them the sanctuary that God wants for them in their relationship. They are to be safe with their spouse, totally exposed without fear of abuse. That can be one reason why divorce is so unsavory. I have seen couples violate that nakedness to find leverage against the other before the civil magistrate and so bring shame to the one they promised to cherish. Failings and foibles are broadcast for all to see.

Against the backdrop of being unashamed, Genesis 3 relates what the doctor looks for in understanding the history of a condition. God had placed Adam and Eve in a garden with the instruction not to eat of a particular tree. We are told that Eve "saw that the tree was good for food, that it was pleasant to the eyes, and a tree desirable to make one wise, [so] she took of its fruit and ate. She also gave to her husband with her, and he ate. Then the eyes of both of them were opened, and they knew that they were naked; and they sewed fig leaves together and made themselves coverings" (Gen. 3:6–7). Death resulted—physical death eventually, but spiritual death immediately. The culprit was not poisoned fruit. It was rebellion against God prompted by the poisoning of their minds through embracing competing counsel to God's. By the transgression of our first parents, nakedness became unnatural. No-shame had given way to shame.

Sin, moral evil, had entered God's good creation. The question is, what would a sin-ravaged world look like? We need only turn the page to Genesis 4 for our answer:

> Now Adam knew Eve his wife, and she conceived and bore Cain, and said, "I have acquired a man from the LORD." Then she bore again, this time his brother Abel. Now Abel was a keeper of sheep, but Cain was a tiller of the ground. And in the process of time it came to pass that Cain brought an offering of the fruit of the ground to the LORD. Abel also brought of the firstborn of his flock and of their fat. And the LORD respected Abel and his offering,

but He did not respect Cain and his offering. And Cain was very angry, and his countenance fell.

So the LORD said to Cain, "Why are you angry? And why has your countenance fallen? If you do well, will you not be accepted? And if you do not do well, sin lies at the door. And its desire is for you, but you should rule over it." (Gen. 4:1–7)

Here we find a historical account that amounts to a case study of what life would look like in a fallen world. We see man in worship. No surprise there. That is how God hardwired those created in His image. Both sons of Adam and Eve bring offerings to present to their Creator, each in keeping with his occupation. Cain, a farmer, brings fruit of the ground. Abel, a shepherd, takes from his flock. The text draws attention to the disparity between the two offerings. Abel brings his best, the fat portions from the firstborn of his flock. The qualification of silence leads us to believe that Cain did not bring his best. The significant contrast is not made so much in terms of what, but why. Hebrews 11:4 explains that Abel's best is the fruit of faith. It is noteworthy that God was already at work in hearts, claiming a people for His own possession, working to counter the sin that usurped devotion and allegiance to God.

God is pleased with Abel's offering. He rejects Cain's. Cain is furious. God tenderly and graciously speaks to Cain to warn him and call him to repent. "So the LORD said to Cain, 'Why are you angry? And why has your countenance fallen? If you do well, will you not be accepted? And if you do not do well, sin lies at the door. And its desire is for you, but you should rule over it'" (Gen. 4:6–7). Cain's prideful, unbridled anger hardens his heart and sets him on a course to disaster. But Cain rejects the counsel of God, a chip off the block of his parents. The result of that rebellion is the murder of his brother.

Such is life in a postfall world. The vulnerability of nakedness would give way to locked doors and guarded outlooks. We see sin intruding on man's relationship with God and with his fellow man, reaching even to the nuclear family. We also see the character and capability of sin resident in the heart of fallen human beings, something we who live on the same side of the fall experience with Cain and Abel. In addition, we are alerted to an enemy crouching at the door of our heart, intent on our spiritual harm.[1]

In this scenario we find the seeds to the self-alienation that can take root in our hearts, providing a breeding ground for guilt. Some have spoken of this as sin affecting four dimensions of relationship: with God (empty worship), with others (murder), with our environment (weeds, thorns), and with our very selves (anger, shame). These seeds give rise to all sorts of symptoms resulting from the infection of sin. Yet in the Seed of the woman, God announced a comprehensive remedy, the One in whom we can rule over sin as God counsels to Cain.

---

1. For more detail on how this scene sets us up for life in a fallen world and the spiritual warfare that becomes part of everyday living, see Stanley D. Gale, *Warfare Witness: Contending with Spiritual Opposition in Everyday Evangelism* (Fearn, Ross-shire, Scotland: Christian Focus, 2005).

Delivered from More Than Sin's Debt

God's gospel is amazing! Planted by His love and grace amid the seeds of guilt and shame (Gen. 3:15), the postfall history that God allowed to continue would feature strife but also would be the womb for the gestation and birth of His promise of life in the giving of His Son in the fullness of time (Gal. 4:4–7). Christ's work would address more than sin's guilt. While forgiveness may be the trophy of God's grace that holds the center position in the display case of His blessings in Christ, it is not the only achievement. The gift box of the gospel contains not only justification but also adoption, sanctification, and glorification—the gamut of Christ's redemption, each addressing a consequence of our fallen condition. Every blessing is nestled in the packing material of grace. The good news heralds the joy of sins forgiven and the promise of new life, abundant and eternal, in Christ Jesus our Lord. It is the gospel *of the kingdom*, the redemptive reign of Christ that encompasses all creation, as far as the curse is found. That kingdom is characterized by righteousness, joy, and peace. And all of it is ours in Christ!

This gospel deals with sin's power and wide-ranging devastation, including the guilt and shame that can plague our hearts. Christ's redeeming work reaches to the debt of sin and also to sin's dominion. Paul spreads before us the scope of Christ's work:

> For the earnest expectation of the creation eagerly waits for the revealing of the sons of God. For the creation was subjected to futility, not willingly, but because of Him who subjected it in hope; because

> the creation itself also will be delivered from the
> bondage of corruption into the glorious liberty of
> the children of God. (Rom. 8:19–21)

In view is nothing less than a new creation, an expression that describes us as believers (2 Cor. 5:17). We can draw on that resurrection life right now. That speaks to deliverance from the corruption of sin and enjoyment of freedom from the guilt and power of sin.

We, as God's children, experience the futility of a fallen world, and we "groan" along with it, under both the weight of its consequences and the anticipation of promised relief. Paul writes, "For we know that the whole creation groans and labors with birth pangs together until now. Not only that, but we also who have the firstfruits of the Spirit, even we ourselves groan within ourselves, eagerly waiting for the adoption, the redemption of our body" (Rom. 8:22–23). We feel the tug of glorification's gravity as the Spirit does His sanctifying work in us, in expectation of our inheritance and experience of its glory. This confidence frames any and every circumstance of our lives: "And we know that all things work together for good to those who love God, to those who are the called according to His purpose" (Rom. 8:28). Romans 8:29 explains the "good" of this assurance as maturation in Christ, conformity to His image. The apostle who went into such detail explaining to us justification, with its jewel of forgiveness, in the early chapters of Romans is the same one who in Romans 6–8 now provides us with a comprehensive overview of the power of the gospel to subdue sin and to transform lives.

In other words, the power of the gospel extends to any and every effect of the fall, including alienation from God, from our fellow man, from our environment, and those effects that wreak havoc in our soul. Anger, worry, depression, envy, greed, shame, and such things create dis-ease in our inner being. The gospel addresses every aspect, giving us strength for today and bright hope for a tomorrow when there will be neither mourning nor crying nor pain, whether they be physical or psychological. Christ's redeeming work, in delivering from the power of sin, is experienced not only in having peace *with* God but in knowing the peace *of* God.

Through His death and resurrection, Jesus brought freedom from sin's guilt *and power*. His work was redeeming, restorative, renewing—both between (in relationship) and within (in our hearts), including whatever may be contributing to the shame and grief of self-blame. We are to know in increasing measure the healing power of the gospel in our lives. That knowledge is a topic of prayer for the apostle Paul:

> Therefore I also, after I heard of your faith in the Lord Jesus and your love for all the saints, do not cease to give thanks for you, making mention of you in my prayers: that the God of our Lord Jesus Christ, the Father of glory, may give to you the spirit of wisdom and revelation in the knowledge of Him, the eyes of your understanding being enlightened; that you may know what is the hope of His calling, what are the riches of the glory of His inheritance in the saints, and what is the exceeding greatness of His power toward us who believe, according to the working of His mighty power which He worked

in Christ when He raised Him from the dead and
seated Him at His right hand in the heavenly places.
(Eph. 1:15–20)

As we are to grow in experiential knowledge of what is ours
in Christ, we are to grow in familiar knowledge of Christ
Himself. Paul prays "that [the Father] would grant you,
according to the riches of His glory, to be strengthened with
might through His Spirit in the inner man, that Christ may
dwell in your hearts through faith" (Eph. 3:16–17).

All this is to say that the gospel does indeed address the
guilt we experience. It does reach to the shame that plagues
a wounded heart. It does speak to the haunting guilt of that
husband and father who finds peace so evasive. The gospel is
God's answer, His means to address the anguish of the soul,
to assuage the nagging assaults of a conscience that gives us
no rest when we blame ourselves. *But that does not mean the
application of the gospel in our sin and shame is administered
by forgiving ourselves.*

I own a toolbox, a red-metal, black-handled, portable
case for my anemic array of tools. What with lost and unre-
turned tools over the years, my assortment is sorely depleted.
Screwdrivers, wrenches, a bent hammer, and, for some
reason, a broken mirror pretty much account for the inven-
tory. Sometimes projects will call for a tool I don't have.
Undaunted, I will try to make do, pressing the wrong tool
into service. More often than not, however, the wrong tool
ends up making things more difficult in the long run.

That is how it can work with trying to forgive ourselves.
We select the wrong implement from the gospel toolbox

because it seems like it might (and even should) do the job. What ends up happening is that by misunderstanding the project and misapplying the means, we end up frustrated and actually doing more harm because we are not addressing the real issue with the right approach. While the gospel does deal with whatever plagues us, it is not through transacting forgiveness with ourselves like we would to address ruptured relationships.

Freedom from Self-Blame

So what can we do when the wrongs we have done torment us, robbing us of peace and joy, drowning us in blame, urging us to usurp the throne to extend the scepter of forgiveness to ourselves? The same healing properties found in gospel forgiveness can be applied to our own hearts not through forgiving ourselves, but through resting more fully in Christ and realizing in greater measure the power of His resurrection at work in us.

Have you ever chided yourself? I do that on the tennis court all the time. "That was dumb. Why go for such a low percentage shot?" "Move your feet; don't reach for the ball." "A drop shot from the baseline! Really?" "Racquet speed. Racquet speed!" These self-admonitions bring to bear the basics and lead to adjustments. They are the tennis equivalent of teaching, reproof, correction, and training in righteousness (2 Tim. 3:16).

We find an example of self-remonstration in Psalms 42 and 43. The psalmist was clearly in pain, racked with inner anguish. His tears had been his food, day and night. He was oppressed of soul and felt himself unable to do anything about it. Sound familiar? That is how the grief-ridden driver felt after that car accident, filled with angst and seemingly impotent to do anything about it. The psalmist acts by challenging himself:

> Why are you cast down, O my soul?
> And why are you disquieted within me?
> Hope in God, for I shall yet praise Him
> For the help of His countenance. (Ps. 42:5; see also 42:11; 43:5)

That admonition becomes his refrain and provides a map to freedom.

The psalmist doesn't engage in self-forgiveness but in self-reproof. He takes himself to task. He recognizes he has lost focus and allowed himself to become hemmed in by the oppression of his soul. But he doesn't look to himself for healing. Rather, he tells himself to look to God, his God, the God who is the hope of his salvation, help for the turmoil that stirs within. He doesn't look inward but instead asks God to fortify and direct him:

> Oh, send out Your light and Your truth!
> Let them lead me;
> Let them bring me to Your holy hill
> And to Your tabernacle.
> Then I will go to the altar of God,
> To God my exceeding joy. (Ps. 43:3–4)

Rather than look to resources within, he reaches out to God for deliverance. He recognizes that God is his ultimate joy and that the longing of his heart was not just for peace but for God Himself. The cries of his sorrows have drowned out his praise for God. He must take the bull by the horns, and he does so by confronting his anguish run amok.

In light of the psalmist's wrestling, what might that husband and father tell himself in the face of his self-blame? It wouldn't be a discussion on forgiving himself. More likely it would be to chastise himself. In the model of the psalmist he might say: "Why are you gripped in anguish, O my soul? Why do you allow guilt to reign as though there were no hope? Why do you allow the enemy to tyrannize you and keep you from the freedom and peace and joy that are yours in Christ? Hope in God. Nestle yourself in His everlasting arms. Find your strength in His all-sufficient grace." That's how we wriggle free of the bonds of self-blame. We remind ourselves of what we know to be true. Through Christ, we are naked before God in our sin and doubts and fears, and we are not ashamed. In Him, we can be completely vulnerable without fear, knowing that a bruised reed He will not break or a smoldering wick snuff out. The guilt of our sin is dealt with in Christ. Darkness is swallowed up in light. We are freed from the power of sin. "I believe; help me in my unbelief." No longer shall the afflicted cry "unclean" to himself or those around him, because his guilt is taken away and his shame removed in the One who entered his misery and bore his blame.

We cannot help but be struck by the candor of the psalmist. He pours out his heart. He lays it on the line. He is honest with himself and real with God. Were he in the place of that guilt-ridden driver, we could well hear him recounting to God in prayer the story of the accident and pouring out the anguish of his soul to Him. He might cry out to God for freedom, healing, and solace. He might challenge himself in his unbelief, pleading for the help of God to work where only He can and in ways only He can. The psalmist gives voice to his despair. He even suggests that God has forgotten him, yet he runs not from God but to Him. The grieving husband and father may believe himself worthy of rejection by God and beyond the reach of the grace of forgiveness, but he will gird his mind against the flood of unbelief by laying in place sandbags of the light and truth of God's Word.

That is the strategy we want to take when we are oppressed in spirit. When we find ourselves in bondage to anything this fallen world has to offer, we want to turn to the gospel of our salvation for liberation. Like the woman plagued with a twelve-year physical affliction turned to Jesus for healing (Luke 8:42–48), so we need to draw near to Him who is willing and able to heal. We want to refresh ourselves in Christ as the living water and hydrate our parched souls with the flowing streams of the gospel of grace.

Girding Our Mind with the Gospel

Just as the psalmist challenges himself, we can challenge ourselves with four resolutions flowing from light and truth in the gospel. First, *confess our sin of exalting self and diminishing Christ.* Pride is like David's son Absalom, laying claim to a throne to which he had no right. We have fallen prey to the enemy's temptation to be as God, absurdly suggesting He does not have our interest at heart and that His ways are inadequate for our need.

In the case of blame harbored against self, our first item for confession is not confession of sin but confession of self—not that self is sin, but self is no savior. That is what we confess as sin—looking to self to save. Rather than dying to self and following Christ, we have turned from the sufficiency of Christ to rely on self. Such confession is not to ourselves, as self-forgiveness would lead us, but to the One we sinned against. He assures us of forgiveness.

But there is more to be gained than diminishment of an inadequate self. A car broke down on a mountain pass. Predawn darkness made it hard to see, and the steady rain did not help. Sheltered under the raised hood of his car, flashlight in hand, the driver tried to determine the problem. After about twenty minutes, fearful and frustrated, he emerged from under the hood. He discovered the morning had dawned and with it one of the most spectacular views he had ever seen. The car remained broken down, but the hope of the new day brightened his spirits and the beauty of the mountain vista filled his eyes and enlivened his heart.

That is the glory of a return to focus on Christ. Rather than preoccupation with the misery of this fallen world, we turn our eyes to Him who has made an end of sin, not only sin's guilt but sin's power and aftermath. We behold the beauty of our Savior Himself. As the hymn writer challenges herself:

O soul, are you weary and troubled?
No light in the darkness you see?
There's light for a look at the Savior,
And life more abundant and free!

Turn your eyes upon Jesus,
Look full in His wonderful face,
And the things of earth will grow strangely dim,
In the light of His glory and grace.[2]

The husband and father besieged by blame must take full refuge in God's sole provision for sin's guilt and power, Christ Jesus the Lord. The survivor's guilt and profound conviction of blaming himself must be answered by resting in Christ. He must harken to the voice of his Lord: "Come to Me, all you who labor and are heavy laden, and I will give you rest. Take My yoke upon you and learn from Me, for I am gentle and lowly in heart, and you will find rest for your souls" (Matt. 11:28–29). It is in the warmth of His love and the light of His truth that the grief and shame of his self-blame will be overwhelmed by the beauty of Christ filling his heart. It is with Him before whom he is totally exposed and thoroughly loved that he will be able to press on.

Second, *stand firm in the Lord against our adversary.* I had just gotten married. Literally. I was in the car with my new bride, having left the reception amid the whoops and hollers of our friends. Our plan was to spend the night locally. I pulled our car, bedecked with streamers and soap-scrawled graffiti, up to the gas pump to fuel it for the travel ahead. In so doing, I clipped another car—nothing major, and not even anything noticeable. The driver of the other vehicle and I had completed our examinations for any damage and were ready to head on our respective ways. That is

---

2. Helen H. Lemmel, "Turn Your Eyes upon Jesus," public domain.

when the troublemaker showed up. He ran up to our cars, saying he had seen the whole thing. If the other driver had any sense, she would call the police and file a report. Who knows? There could be all sorts of unseen damage. Would the insurance pay without a police report? I was getting more unnerved by the minute. Thankfully, the other driver saw through the absurdity of the instigator, and we parted company on good terms.

The Bible alerts us to a spiritual adversary who would rob us of the peace that is ours in Christ and mislead us in finding that peace. We are told not to be unaware of this tormentor's schemes. It is interesting that the apostle Paul issues this alert in the context of grievance and forgiveness. "Therefore I urge you to reaffirm your love to him. For to this end I also wrote, that I might put you to the test, whether you are obedient in all things. Now whom you forgive anything, I also forgive. For if indeed I have forgiven anything, I have forgiven that one for your sakes in the presence of Christ, lest Satan should take advantage of us; for we are not ignorant of his devices" (2 Cor. 2:8–11).

What that means is we need to adopt God's strategies and take up the weapons He provides for the conduct of spiritual warfare inherent in living for Christ in this fallen world.[3] The strategy Paul gives us is *to stand*:

> Finally, my brethren, be strong in the Lord and in
> the power of His might. Put on the whole armor of

---

3. For exposition of Satan's tactics and how God empowers and equips us to deal with them, see Stanley D. Gale, *What Is Spiritual Warfare?* (Phillipsburg, N.J.: P&R, 2010).

God, that you may be able to stand against the wiles
of the devil. For we do not wrestle against flesh and
blood, but against principalities, against powers,
against the rulers of the darkness of this age, against
spiritual hosts of wickedness in the heavenly places.
Therefore take up the whole armor of God, that you
may be able to withstand in the evil day, and having
done all, to stand.

Stand therefore. (Eph. 6:10–14)

Our adversary would lead us into ourselves to find rest
through efforts at untying the bonds of our guilt. Our Advocate invites us to Himself to find rest in His presence, in His
deliverance, in His healing, by His hand. The answer is not
in finding a way to forgive ourselves, but in finding the way,
the truth, and the life. In Him are bound up all those things
for which our heart longs—peace, joy, forgiveness, freedom,
refreshment, strength. He suffered the penalty of our guilt.
He bore the reproach of our shame.

Recognizing that spiritual warfare is afoot, the husband and father gripped in guilt must stand firm in Christ's
grace against self-accusation, stand firm in Christ's truth
against false counsel that seems right to self, and stand firm
in Christ's power against self-inability to overcome. His
approach must not be to assert self but to humble himself
before God, that He may lift him up. Satan will accuse by
heaping guilt on his plagued conscience and tormenting his
soul with guilt. Against this accusation, he must resist the
bondage and live in the freedom that is his in Christ. Let
him hear the words of the hymn:

> When Satan tempts me to despair
> And tells me of the guilt within,
> Upward I look and see Him there
> Who made an end of all my sin.
> Because the sinless Savior died,
> My sinful soul is counted free;
> For God the Just is satisfied
> To look on Him and pardon me,
> To look on Him and pardon me.[4]

When Satan impresses on him his powerlessness to overcome, let him stand in the resurrection power of Christ, through whom he can do all things. When Satan suggests ways that have a semblance of truth, let him stand firm on the Word of God, with this charter:

> As you therefore have received Christ Jesus the Lord, so walk in Him, rooted and built up in Him and established in the faith, as you have been taught, abounding in it with thanksgiving.
>
> Beware lest anyone cheat you through philosophy and empty deceit, according to the tradition of men, according to the basic principles of the world, and not according to Christ. (Col. 2:6–8)

In and through all these, that husband and father must pray always in the Spirit, with all prayer and supplication, in complete and continual dependence on God (see Eph. 6:18).

---

4. Charitie Lees Bancroft, "Before the Throne of God Above," public domain.

God's counsel to Cain, that he not let sin rule over him but instead rule over it, points to Jesus Christ in the gospel.

Third, *rest in the peace of Christ.* Jesus extends these words of comfort and empowerment to those who know Him: "Peace I leave with you, My peace I give to you; not as the world gives do I give to you. Let not your heart be troubled, neither let it be afraid" (John 14:27). Jesus directs any whose hearts are troubled to Himself, where He offers a peace neither found in the world nor that the world has a right to. The despondent driver swallowed up in shame must pursue the path of peace laid out in passages like Philippians 4:4–9:

> Rejoice in the Lord always. Again I will say, rejoice!
>
> Let your gentleness be known to all men. The Lord is at hand.
>
> Be anxious for nothing, but in everything by prayer and supplication, with thanksgiving, let your requests be made known to God; and the peace of God, which surpasses all understanding, will guard your hearts and minds through Christ Jesus.
>
> Finally, brethren, whatever things are true, whatever things are noble, whatever things are just, whatever things are pure, whatever things are lovely, whatever things are of good report, if there is any virtue and if there is anything praiseworthy—meditate on these things. The things which you learned and received and heard and saw in me, these do, and the God of peace will be with you. (Phil. 4:4–9)

Notice that the path to peace runs through a mind that takes captive every thought to conform to Christ.[5] It lays out a path that offers peace that surpasses all understanding and that leads to the God of peace Himself. That driver must bring his mind to dwell on truth that builds up, much as we saw with the self-reminders and self-remonstrations of the psalmist in Psalm 42. This self-admonition is not a onetime fix but a continual application of God's truth, like keeping both hands on the steering wheel while traveling the road of life in this fallen world.

I led a seminar on forgiveness. In it I explained from Psalm 42 that the psalmist met anguish of soul not by self-forgiveness but by self-reproof, chastising himself for languishing in despair and not hoping in God. After the seminar a young man approached me and asked how we keep self-reproof from falling back into self-blame. His question does make sense, because reproof and blame share a certain negative self-assessment and can lead to a downward spiral.

My answer was twofold. First, self-reproof is not directed to what we blame ourselves for but to our dealing with that blame in a wrong way. We don't reprove ourselves for our fault—that feeds the self-blame. Rather, we reprove ourselves for taking the wrong *approach* to the self-blame. We reprove ourselves for looking to self rather than to the Savior for strength, solace, and security. We challenge ourselves

---

5. Specific examples on how to follow this path of peace can be found in chapter 4 of Stanley D. Gale, *A Vine-Ripened Life: Spiritual Fruitfulness through Abiding in Christ* (Grand Rapids: Reformation Heritage Books, 2014).

for seeking remedy in ourselves rather than in God, through our internal machinations rather than through the gospel. Second, we need to recognize the spiritual warfare afoot. Satan points out our sin to drive us to despair. The Spirit highlights our sin to drive us to Christ. Self-reproof is not a state to be lingered in, like some sort of self-flagellation, but a turnabout that takes us to Christ for the healing, freedom, peace, and strength bound up in Him. Chastising ourselves is not the self-abuse of berating ourselves, like self-blame does. Instead, it defies the taunts of Satan to find the presence and power of Christ in the gospel.

Finally, *press on in faith*. Grief and shame can sideline us, leaving us barely able to function. But God bids that we run the race set before us, unfettered by shame's weight and unhindered by sin's snare.

> Therefore we also, since we are surrounded by so great a cloud of witnesses, let us lay aside every weight, and the sin which so easily ensnares us, and let us run with endurance the race that is set before us, looking unto Jesus, the author and finisher of our faith, who for the joy that was set before Him endured the cross, despising the shame, and has sat down at the right hand of the throne of God.
>
> For consider Him who endured such hostility from sinners against Himself, lest you become weary and discouraged in your souls. (Heb. 12:1–3)

We run with eyes of faith that perceive unseen realities (Heb. 11:1). We are to fix our gaze on Christ, our help and hope, our strength and shield. Our prayer may well be, "I do believe; help me in my unbelief," but we press on. Guilt and shame are obstacles to be overcome in Christ and hindrances to be tossed off through consideration of all that we have in Him: "I can do all things through Christ who strengthens me" (Phil. 4:13).

The husband and father overcome with grief cannot languish on the sidelines but must return to the race, tossing aside every encumbrance and the sin that so easily entangles, looking not to self but to Christ. That race is not run in a single bound, but step by step, one foot in front of the other in the direction of Christ—Christ for me, Christ before me. The course we run has been determined by the purpose of God for us. He does not give us inclines more than we can bear or seas too rough for us to navigate, including those events of our lives that produce grief, blame, and shame. Christ is not only our focus but He is with us, His presence to cheer and to guide.

Only in Christ, through whom we can do all things, do we find the power to press on, the grace to overcome, and the resolve to take hold of the peace and joy that are ours in Him. Whatever bondage or oppression from sin's consequence that we may experience in this fallen world, our Lord urges us to take courage. Why? Jesus explains: "These things I have spoken to you, that in Me you may have peace. In the world you will have tribulation; but be of good cheer, I have overcome the world" (John 16:33). Believers are given two certainties while in this age: afflictions and ability to overcome them in Christ.

Redeeming Guilt

The quest to forgive ourselves is a journey to find freedom from sin's guilt that lays siege to our conscience. Often, that journey leads us into self rather than to Christ and the power of the gospel to deal with sin's guilt and shame. We endeavor to let go of the blame that haunts us by forgiving ourselves rather than finding ourselves in Christ and knowing the liberating power of His resurrection.

We've seen how we can go about knowing that power in greater measure, but God has more for us than escape from the bondage of self-accusation. The experience of guilt is a natural reaction to sin, just as Jesus's tears at the tomb of Lazarus were a natural reaction to the intrusion of death into relationships and God's good creation. In fact, guilt is intensified by a supple conscience no longer seared by sin's hardening. Aversion to sin plagues us all the more when we see it glaring in our lives, as would a crumpled fender on a newly purchased car. The guilt of our being an accessory to wrong is enhanced. And that can be a good thing.

When I served as a hospital chaplain, I met a young woman. Let's call her Alice. Alice was a joy to spend time with, full of good humor and experience that belied her nineteen years. She was in the hospital because of bedsores. Alice had been born with spina bifida and was confined to a wheelchair. She had no feeling from the waist down. When most of us get uncomfortable sitting for too long, we shift in our seats. Alice didn't know when to do that because she would not feel the discomfort. As a result, her skin would break down and create sores that would sometimes open all the way to the bone.

Pain can be useful to us. Discomfort can be a red flag calling for our attention, enabling us to do something about it. Alice did not have that sensation. As a result, her body gave her no feedback when bad things were happening to it.

Guilt can be viewed as moral pain. The agitations of a supple conscience are like stimulated nerve endings that hurt and call for attention. On the one hand, in justification we can numb that pain of transgression through the analgesic of grace that removes the guilt that shackles us before the judgment seat of God. On the other hand, by God's sanctifying grace we can meet head-on the miseries of remaining sin to find relief, freedom, strength, and healing in Jesus Christ. Dealing with guilt through justification frees us *from* sin's condemnation, but dealing with guilt in our sanctification frees us *for* knowing abundant life in Jesus Christ.

Rather than looking to forgive ourselves in response to guilt's distresses in our hearts, we would be better served to benefit from that feedback to examine ourselves for pockets of gospel resistance. We want to enlist the help of the Holy Spirit as we pray,

> Search me, O God, and know my heart;
> Try me, and know my anxieties;
> And see if there is any wicked way in me,
> And lead me in the way everlasting. (Ps. 139:23–24)

In other words, instead of seeing guilt as something to escape, we want to redeem that guilt by examining its source for our growth in grace. In that examination we might discover resistance to God's forgiveness, pockets of pride, strains of unbelief, or areas where self reigns rather than Christ.

The road to sanctification wends through all sorts of road and weather conditions that call on us to bring the light of God's truth to bear, including those high beams that enable us to negotiate the darkest of conditions. The heavy self-blame of the husband and father we saw earlier should not lead him to run from his guilt but to run to it, taking stock of it and taking solace in the comfort of the gospel. He needs not just to chastise himself for not hoping in God, but he must look to God to understand where he needs to die to self and live to Christ. That means redeeming the guilt, benefitting from its cries for attention, and addressing it with the means of grace provided by God, that he might live in glorious freedom as an adopted son of God.

There are those who contend we are audacious not to forgive ourselves if God has forgiven us. Who do we think we are? That sentiment has a ring of rightness about it, but it misses the point. Forgiving ourselves is not something we are to pursue at all. To use a baseball analogy, it is like wondering if I should bunt or swing for the fences while I'm standing as a runner on second base. Forgiveness reflects a different part of the game. We deal with nagging guilt and the continuing presence of sin's effects not by forgiving ourselves, but by freeing ourselves from the enslaving power of sin and shame. God's strategy to find that freedom is in realizing the liberating power of the resurrected Christ to overcome. Self has figured prominently in passages such as Psalm 42, but not as a source of hope. Rather, self is taken to task that hope might be found in God and help bound up in His provision.

Let this be our prayer for ourselves and for our fellow believers reeling from the plague of sin in any way:

> Now may the God of hope fill you with all joy and peace in believing, that you may abound in hope by the power of the Holy Spirit. (Rom. 15:13)

Discovery Questions

Reflect: Have you ever felt the need to forgive yourself? How did you handle it?

1. How did our hearts become a breeding ground for guilt and self-condemnation?

2. What blessings other than justification does Christ's redeeming work bring to you?

3. What does it mean that the power of the gospel reaches not only to sin's debt but also to sin's dominion?

4. How can the prayers of Ephesians 1:15–21 and 3:16–19 be brought to bear against shame and self-blame?

5. What approach do we find in Psalms 42 and 43 for addressing self-blame and its manifestations?

6. What strategy does the gospel of life, power, and freedom in Christ offer that runs counter to the effort of forgiving ourselves?

7. In what way does self-blame provide opportunity for growth in the grace and knowledge of our Lord Jesus Christ?